Praise

Praying the Scripture

Jodie Berndt has provided a tangible way to utilize the most powerful tool we have for equipping our children—namely, prayer. With guided meditations for every occasion to shower provision and blessing over your teen, this book is one that all parents need.

>REBEKAH LYONS, bestselling author of
>*Rhythms of Renewal* and *You are Free*

Don't miss out on praying these Scriptures for your teens. It is the greatest gift you can give them. It will change their lives!

>FERN NICHOLS, founder and president,
>Moms in Prayer International

Jodie Berndt's books have been a *very* special gift in our lives. Her stories keep us smiling, even on the toughest days, and remind us that we're not alone in our struggle to parent well. Jodie points us to God's Word and the power of prayer for specific situations, often when we seem to need it most. If I had to recommend only one book to parents who feel lost during their child's teen years, it would be this one!

>MIKE CUNNION, father of five boys and
>CEO of Remedy Health Media

As a mother in the thick of raising three teenage sons, I highly recommend *Praying the Scriptures for Your Teens*. Once our kids hit those challenging teen years, the most powerful thing we can do is love them like crazy and then open up the Word and pray, pray, pray. I believe Jodie Berndt's book is one of the most helpful and practical parenting resources you'll ever put your hands on.

>LISA JACOBSON, author and founder
>of Club31Women.com

With four teens under my roof, I can't think of a better book for my nightstand. Prayer, Scripture, and story intertwined, this book is for both the hard crucible and the beautiful highs of raising children.

SARA HAGERTY, bestselling author of *Adore* and *Unseen*

You'll laugh, cry, and identify with Jodie. She's real. Best of all, these pages will give you a strategy and a hope.

SUSAN ALEXANDER YATES, author of *Cousin Camp*

This is an easy-to-use, yet incredibly effective guide for parents who want to use to the fullest extent the two most powerful tools in parenting—prayer and Scripture.

JOE WHITE, president, Kanakuk Kamps

Trained in the trenches of praying her own children through their teen years (and beyond), Jodie Berndt's wisdom reads like pure encouragement from a gentle mentor. Intensely practical, honest, and relatable, *Praying the Scriptures for Your Teens* is far more than a book; it's a valuable tool for anyone who wants to be a warrior, a faithful intercessor in praying God's Word over the teens in their lives. What a vital resource to guide us as we pray our teens through one of the most intense seasons of their lives!

KATIE WESTENBERG, author of *I Choose Brave*

"Parenting improves your prayer life" was one of my mother's wisest insights about prayer. When I became a parent, my prayer life improved dramatically. *Praying the Scriptures for Your Teens* provides the tools we need to parent and pray with confidence. I am relieved when I remember that God loves our teens more than we do and knows them better than we do. They are never out of his reach.

LISA ROBERTSON, author of *The Path of Life*

Praying the Scriptures
for Your Teens

Also by Jodie Berndt

Celebration of Miracles

Praying the Scriptures for Your Adult Children

Praying the Scriptures for Your Children, 20th Anniversary Edition

Praying the Scriptures for Your Adult Children
Study Guide (available at jodieberndt.com)

Praying the Scriptures for Your Children, 20th Anniversary
Edition Study Guide (available at jodieberndt.com)

Praying the Scriptures for Your Teens

Opening the Door *for* God's Provision *in* Their Lives

UPDATED AND EXPANDED

JODIE BERNDT

ZONDERVAN BOOKS

ZONDERVAN BOOKS

Praying the Scriptures for Your Teens
Copyright © 2007, 2021 by Jodie Berndt

Published in Grand Rapids, Michigan, by Zondervan. Zondervan is a registered trademark of The Zondervan Corporation, L.L.C., a wholly owned subsidiary of HarperCollins Christian Publishing, Inc.

Requests for information should be addressed to customercare@harpercollins.com.

Zondervan titles may be purchased in bulk for educational, business, fundraising, or sales promotional use. For information, please email SpecialMarkets@Zondervan.com.

ISBN 978-0-310-36199-2 (audio)

Library of Congress Cataloging-in-Publication Data

Names: Berndt, Jodie, author.
Title: Praying the scriptures for your teens : opening the door for God's provision in their lives / Jodie Berndt.
Description: Grand Rapids : Zondervan, 2021. | Includes bibliographical references. | Summary: "Jodie Berndt offers hundreds of biblically based prayers, so you can pray specifically--and expectant-ly--about the things that matter most to you and your teen. This expanded edition features updated content on issues like pornography, addiction, self-harm, anxiety, rebellion, technology use, dealing with disappointment, and more"-- Provided by publisher.
Identifiers: LCCN 2020045497 (print) | LCCN 2020045498 (ebook) | ISBN 9780310361985 (trade paperback) | ISBN 9780310541004 (ebook)
Subjects: LCSH: Bible--Devotional literature. | Mothers--Prayers and devotions. | Christian teenagers --Religious life.
Classification: LCC BV4847 .B463 2021 (print) | LCC BV4847 (ebook) | DDC 242/.63--dc23
LC record available at https://lccn.loc.gov/2020045497
LC ebook record available at https://lccn.loc.gov/2020045498

Cover design: Curt Diepenhorst
Cover photo: Lina Stling / Getty Images
Author photo: Natalie Puls Photography
Interior design: Kristy Edwards

Printed in the United States of America
24 25 26 27 28 LBC 24 23 22 21 20

For Hillary, Annesley, Virginia, and Robbie Jr.—

He who began a good work in you will carry it on to
completion until the day of Christ Jesus.
Philippians 1:6

I love you.
And I love watching God's good work
in your lives.

Contents

Part 4: Praying for Your Teen's
Victory over Temptation

Part 5: Praying about Everything

Foreword

There is an anonymous saying that dates back to World War I that goes like this: "We have no atheists in the trenches." In a similar vein, I'd offer, "We have no parents of a teen who don't pray." As Ann and I had the honor of raising three boys (who are adults now), we didn't need a prayer list to remind us to pray, or what to pray, as we daily lifted them before the Father.

It's not that, "I've tried everything else, guess now I'll pray." Rather, the greatest gift we can give our teen children is to pray daily for them.

If your child has entered their teen years, you are well aware that the environment they are growing up in is fraught with danger. Nothing in our current culture encourages your teen toward deepening their relationship with Jesus. Even without leaving your home, they can be exposed to the violence and sex of movies and video games, music with words that repulse us, pornography at the touch of their finger, and a smartphone that keeps them "connected" but carries with it comparisons, pressures and stress, feelings of inadequacy/not being included/not measuring up, FOMO, and "social bullying" that we never knew in our teen years.

Jodie Berndt provides here a guide to your prayers. When

you've grown tired of praying the same words or you've run out of words, Jodie introduces us to the power that comes with praying God's Word over and around our teens.

Without necessarily meaning to, this is really a parenting book. Using true-life stories and giving practical help, Jodie tackles many of the challenges teens face and offers real encouragement.

As parents, we love our children, provide them with every opportunity to succeed, advocate for them and stand up for them, protect them, speak truth to them, cry with them when they hurt, laugh with them over the funny things of life, and celebrate with them even over little things—I could go on and on. In short, we fight for them.

The apostle Paul writes in Ephesians 6:12, "Our struggle is not against flesh and blood [the things of this world], but against the rulers, against the authorities, against the powers of this dark world and against the spiritual forces of evil in the heavenly realms." We enter into this battle by praying. Jesus said, "No one can come to me unless the Father who sent me draws them" (John 6:44). We beg for our kids' hearts by praying. *Praying the Scriptures for Your Teens* equips us to pray. I could not commend it to you more passionately.

Ty Saltzgiver, former Young Life US field director
and bestselling author of *My First 30 Quiet Times*

Whack-a-Mole Parenting

"If you remain in me and my words remain in you,
ask whatever you wish, and it will be done for you."
John 15:7

When I was working on the original edition of this book, the folks at Zondervan let me know they were meeting to discuss the cover design. "Do you," they asked, "have any specific ideas or input to contribute?"

"Well," I said, "if you were to poll my friends who are raising teens right now, they'd probably tell you to just go ahead and make the cover black."

"Black?"

"Yes, but you could put a ray of light cutting across the darkness to symbolize God's intervention in our desperate lives."

I was kidding—sort of. Ty Saltzgiver (the guy who wrote the foreword and who spent more than forty years hanging out with adolescents in his work with Young Life) taught me that you are never "just kidding." There's always a kernel of truth in there somewhere. And in this case, Ty was right: My friends and I knew that God loved our kids and that he was at work in their lives, but there were plenty of days when our hearts just felt ... dark. Our spirits were heavy. The list of what-ifs and worries—safety on the road, substance abuse, eating disorders, anxiety, sexual purity, spiritual doubt—seemed limitless. No sooner would we finish praying about one thing than another would, like a crazed whack-a-mole, pop its head out of the hole.

Robbie and I had four kids in six years (which translated, I think, to four teens over thirteen consecutive years), and during the time it took to write and publish this book, we prayed our way through almost every topic you'll find in these pages. I even found myself wondering whether God—in that Godlike way of his—allowed some specific challenges to manifest themselves in our family just to remove any lingering threads of self-sufficiency, pride, or judgmental attitudes I might have tried to hang on to had I not found myself in the parenting gutter so many times.

Case in point: As I was working on the chapter about praying for our teens' attire and thinking about the importance of modesty, God reminded me of the time that our daughter and two of her friends went to a rock concert dressed—unbeknownst to us—in skimpy shirts they had made themselves. Lest you think I should have been proud of a teen who could sew, I'll just go ahead and tell you that the girls used staples, not thread. And the shimmery gold fabric they thought looked so fetching? They had ransacked it from a neighbor's nativity set.

Wrong, on so many levels.

Our kids' fashion choices are but one of an untold number of things we may find ourselves praying about. There are other topics—so many topics—that you won't find in the table of contents, not because I didn't think they were important or because we didn't walk down those roads, but simply because—to borrow an explanation from the apostle John as he wrote about the mighty works Jesus did—"If every one of them were written down, I suppose that even the whole world would not have room for the books that would be written."[1] Academic struggles, sibling relationships, teen pregnancy, parental divorce, the loss of a loved one . . . if you find yourself—if you find your teen—coming up against one of these challenging places, know this: There is no need we will face that God has not already thought of, and provided for, in his Word. He understands. He's been there. He is there with you still.

And he invites you—he invites us—to anchor our trust in his promises.

If you read *Praying the Scriptures for Your Children*—better yet, if you prayed your way through that book—you know that God's Word is powerful and effective. You know that it does not return empty but always accomplishes God's purposes and desires. And perhaps more than anything else, you know that it holds the key to endurance and hope.[2]

Which, in a nutshell, is what this book is all about.

As a mom, I've always considered prayer to be a vital part of my job description (as someone once said, "If you're not praying for your child, who is?"), but when I began using Scripture as the basis for my prayers—taking the actual words in the Bible and using them to shape my requests—I found that prayer became less of a "duty" and more of an adventure. When I read my Bible, I would discover phrases and promises that I could pray over my kids. My conversations with God began to take on a whole new dimension. Gone were the repetitive and sometimes—dare I say it?—boring petitions for generic blessings and protection; my prayers became interesting and creative and infused with a fresh kind of power. I shouldn't have been surprised—God's word is, after all, active and alive[3]—but I wasn't prepared for the depth of connection that came with speaking to God in the language he first spoke to me, nor could I have anticipated the fulfillment, joy, and confidence that came with tapping into words that had been conceived and shaped in God's heart!

My desire in writing this book is to give you that same sense of connection, fulfillment, and joy. I want you to pray with confidence, knowing that when you come before God, you will receive mercy and find grace for your every need—for your *teen's* every need.[4]

In the pages to come, you'll meet parents who have wrestled and prayed their way through everything from their teen's questions about God to issues like loneliness, anger, parties, and relationships. You'll meet teens—musicians and athletes, popular kids and loners, churchgoers and rebels—and see how God has worked in their lives. And although I've often changed names or small details to protect their identities, all of the people in this book are real.

They are also people who believe that God is still writing our stories. They know—as I do—that when God delivers their teen from the concern or crisis *du jour*, the next one might be only a history class, a party, or a boyfriend away. This reality—that our kids are still under construction—actually served as a bit of a stumbling block for some of the parents I interviewed. Knowing that their teens had hurdles yet to cross, they were reluctant to discuss the good things that God had already accomplished, lest they appear to be counting their chickens too soon. Not only that, but one mother I spoke with worried that if she talked about what God had done in her daughter's life—the answers to prayer she had experienced—it could look as though she was being boastful.

As I wondered about these concerns, God directed me to 1 Samuel 7, the passage where the threat of a Philistine assault has the Israelites shaking in their sandals. "Do not stop crying out to the LORD our God for us," the Israelites beg Samuel, "that he may rescue us from the hand of the Philistines."

Samuel prays, God answers, and the Israelites slaughter the bad guys. Afterward, Samuel takes a stone and sets it up not far from the battlefield. He names the stone "Ebenezer"—which means "stone of help"—saying, "Thus far the LORD has helped us."[5]

Did Samuel think that the Philistines had been banished forever? I doubt it; they were a constant source of trouble, both before and after this victory. But did it stop him from thanking God or from giving him public glory? Not at all! Samuel built his Ebenezer as a marker—a sign of remembrance—so that generations to come would be able to see it and say, "God did that."

As praying parents, we need to do the same thing. Rather than cower in worry or fear over our particular Philistines and the threat of what they might do in the future, we need to stop and thank God for what he has already done. When God works in answer to our prayers, we need to raise our own Ebenezers, acknowledging his provision "thus far"—and counting on him to help us in the future.

The verse at the beginning of this introduction—John 15:7— says that if we remain in Christ and his words remain in us, we can ask whatever we wish, and it will be done for us. That's a beautiful promise, but it's only part of the story. In the very next verse, Jesus explains the reason he wants us to pray: "This is to my Father's glory," he says, "that you bear much fruit, showing yourselves to be my disciples."

"The true purpose in prayer," wrote R. A. Torrey, "is that God may be glorified in the answer."[6] I believe that—but I also know how easy it can be for contemporary parents (well, *this* parent at least) to glorify or idolize our children. Not overtly, of course, but when we center our thoughts on our kids—either because they have made us so *proud* or because they have made us so *anxious*—we inadvertently elbow God out of the picture.

So let's not. Let's release our teens to God and pray with thanksgiving—no matter what the present circumstances are or the future what-ifs might look like—knowing that God has everything under control. Let's pray with a heart that desires, above anything else, to bring honor and glory to God.

Will there be times when our hearts feel dark and our spirits are heavy? Of course. But from where I sit now, praying four all-grown-up children through the whack-a-mole issues in their young adult lives, I will tell you that I am glad the original edition of this book was not covered in black. And I'm even more glad, as I look back over my kids' teen years and see the fingerprints of God's faithfulness, that the new cover looks like it does. To me, it speaks of hope, light, and the power of God's Word to open doors in our teens' lives.

In his letter to the Colossians, Paul asked them to pray that God would open a door so that he and his companions could proclaim the mystery of Christ.[7]

As you open this book, may God open a door for his Word in

your heart, equipping you to proclaim his praise from generation to generation.[8] May he use you and your prayers to accomplish his purposes in the lives of the people you love.

Part 1

Praying for Your Teen's Relationships

Chapter 1

Praying for Your Teen's Relationship with Christ

*So then, just as you received Christ Jesus as Lord,
continue to live your lives in him, rooted and built
up in him, strengthened in the faith as you were
taught, and overflowing with thankfulness.*
Colossians 2:6–7

After dropping off our combined eight children on the first day of school, my friend Anne and I decided to stop for a cup of coffee. We headed to Starbucks, where we were delighted to run into a friend—let's call her Darcy—we hadn't seen in a while.

"How old are your kids now?" Darcy asked.

When she learned that Anne and I had four teens between us, Darcy broke into a huge smile. "I remember those days!" she cried. "And I want you to meet my friend Patty."

Darcy pulled Patty into our circle. "Our kids grew up together," she explained, "and we stayed in touch, even after our family moved—and then her son married my daughter!"

"Remember when we took that vacation to St. Simon's Island?" Patty prompted.

"Oh, yes!" Darcy said. "Our kids were teens—and you can imagine the kinds of things that were weighing on our hearts. Patty and I snuck off one day and found this little chapel where we could pray. We spent the entire morning pouring out our hearts to the Lord, like it says in Lamentations 2:19, lifting up our hands to him for the lives of our children."

"We prayed for each of them by name, one at a time—" Patty added.

"—and we never dreamed that two of them would grow up and get married to each other!" Darcy finished.

As Darcy and Patty continued to reminisce, Anne and I exchanged a look. I knew what she was thinking: we needed to get away and take time to pray for our kids, one by one.

"Let's do it tomorrow," Anne suggested.

The next day we met at the beach, right next to the big wooden cross that marks the spot where the Jamestown colonists landed, thirteen years before the Pilgrims arrived. We poured out our hearts, and then—just as we finished—the sky poured down rain. We snatched up our prayer journals and bolted for the car.

"We need to do this again!" Anne said, laughing.

"Yes," I agreed, "just as soon as my Bible dries out."

I'm grateful to God for how he "set up" our meeting with Darcy and Patty that day. Their friendship and their commitment to praying together (even in the hard and vulnerable seasons) stands as a testimony to the power of unified prayer.[1] If you don't already have a friend you can confide in and pray with, ask God to give you a trusted prayer partner. First, though, I want to share one of Darcy's stories with you . . .

∿ ∿ ∿

Darcy and Wayne loved the fact that their kids
were friends with all sorts of people. Rather
than hang out in any particular clique or group
at school, their son Mark enjoyed being with
the prepsters, the church kids, the skaters,
and—perhaps most of all—the athletes. As
a six-year-old boy, Mark had met his idol,
Michael Jordan, and his greatest desire was to
follow in the basketball player's footsteps.

By the time Mark hit high school, it looked as though his
dream might come true. A star player on the school's basketball
team, he set his sights on playing Division I ball. In addition to
his athletic talent, he seemed to have everything a teen boy could
wish for—a cute girlfriend, a pack of guys to run around with,
and parents who truly loved him.

In Wayne and Darcy's mind, though, something was missing. Mark had been raised in the church, and at the age of five,
he had asked to be baptized. Once he got his driver's license,
he drove all over town, picking up kids and bringing them to a
nondenominational youth group, where many of them came to
faith in Christ. Deep down, though, Darcy knew her son was not
walking closely with God. Basketball was the only thing he really
cared about.

"Make him a man," Wayne prayed day in and day out. "Make
him a man of God."

Darcy wanted to believe God would answer that prayer, but—
looking at Mark's friends (many of whom were making some
seriously bad choices) and his total lack of interest in anything
remotely connected to church (except for the socially oriented

youth group)—she didn't see how it could happen. And when Mark graduated from high school and got a job busing tables at a local nightclub, Darcy feared he'd slip even further away.

"He can't work in that horrible place!" she said to Wayne. "You've got to do something."

"He got a summer job like we asked. Don't worry," Wayne said. "He'll be fine."

One night, some of Darcy and Wayne's friends—a family in town for the weekend—decided to visit the nightclub. "Let's go say hi to Mark at work," one of the college-aged visitors suggested. "We can dance; it'll be fun!"

The group trooped off to the night spot, only to find it closed for the evening, with no sign of Mark. Darcy tried to hide her concern, but when her son still hadn't returned by three in the morning—four hours after his curfew—she was frantic.

Once again, Wayne provided a calming presence. "He'll be back," he said.

Mark did come back—and found himself facing his father's wrath. "You need to stay by my side for the rest of the weekend so you can be with our guests. After that, you're moving out."

"What?" Mark asked.

"You heard me. You can't live in our house if you're going to show such total disregard for our rules. You're heading off to college in six weeks. I'm sure you'll find someplace to live until then."

Mark moved into an apartment with a couple of guys. Had Darcy known what he was eating—leftover scraps from the tables he bused—she might have worried even more than she initially did, but she understood the importance of being united with her husband and agreed that making her son face the consequences of his actions was, in the end, the right thing to do.

PRAYER PRINCIPLE

When you have to make hard choices in
parenting, ask God to give you courage and (if
you are married) seek unity with your spouse.

Mark hit the college campus without his hoped-for scholarship, but he landed a spot on the basketball team as a walk-on. Meanwhile, Darcy continued to pray for her son's relationship with the Lord. She would go into his empty bedroom, put her hands on his bed, and cry out to God. "Let Mark know how much you love him," she prayed. "Let him grasp how wide and long and high and deep your love is—and cause him to surrender his life to you."[2]

She also sent care packages to Mark's dorm—including stacks of Christian music CDs that she hoped he would play. If nothing else, she knew the CDs would make him at least *think* about God—and serve as a reminder that his mother was praying.

PRAYER PRINCIPLE

Pray in your teen's bedroom when they're
not home. Ask the Holy Spirit to show
them how much they are loved.

Mark's first year at school passed without incident. He loved playing basketball and seemed to get along well with the other players. During the fall of his second year, however, Mark called home, and Darcy could tell he was upset.

"You're playing basketball at a Division I school, right?" Darcy asked.

"Right."

"And you're dating a beautiful girl?"

"Right."

"And you're not all that happy."

"Right."

"Well," Darcy sighed, "I don't know what else to say, other than what Daddy and I have always told you. Until you really surrender your life to the Lord, you will never find the peace and the joy that you're looking for."

Mark didn't say much, and so Darcy continued. "I love you, son. You know I do. But this is a decision you need to make for yourself; I can't do it for you."

She hung up the telephone, thinking she'd said the same thing to Mark—that he needed to give his life completely to Jesus—a hundred times before. Would he ever listen?

For reasons even Mark does not fully understand, that phone call—and the calm assurance in his mother's voice—served as a turning point in his life. And as he looked around and saw several top athletes getting drunk every night with nothing to show for it, he realized that the life of a basketball star—at least one who wasn't walking with the Lord—was not one he wanted.

Mark decided to transfer to a college closer to home. It wasn't a Division I school, but he could still play basketball and figured a change of scenery could help settle his restless heart. He moved in with his parents—but things like getting up early on Sunday morning to go to church with them were definitely *not* in his plans.

"You can't *make* me go," Mark said, stubbornly. "I'm in college now, and I'm an adult. I want to live my own life."

Wayne's tough love showed its face again. "You can live your own life when you can pay your own way. If you want to live here, you have to go to church. I don't care if you lie down on the floor in the back and go to sleep. You *need* to go with us on Sunday."

Grudgingly, Mark went—but if he liked the music or the sermons, he didn't say so. Darcy and Wayne did the only thing they knew to do: they kept praying.

And then one Sunday, when the minister invited people to come forward if they wanted to surrender their lives to the Lord, they saw their son walk down the aisle.

Poised for Prayer

Mark grew up to lead one of the largest, most culturally and racially diverse churches in the country. Considering how her son is wired, Darcy sees his life as a tangible manifestation of the Ephesians 2:10 promise, that we are created in Christ Jesus to do good works, which God prepared in advance for us to do. God used the bits and pieces of Mark's background—from his love for sports to his comfort level with all kinds of people—to equip him for works of service that build up the body of Christ.[3]

Looking back on their sometimes heartbreaking journey, Darcy admits she and Wayne did a lot of things wrong. "But we hung in there," she says, "and we kept pointing Mark toward the Lord.

"I know you can't force a relationship with God on your children," she continues, "but you can try to get them in an atmosphere—such as in a Bible-believing church—where their hearts and eyes might be opened. God's word will not return empty.[4] Mark is a living testimony to that truth.

"I never would have believed it, but our son has become—just like his daddy prayed—a man of God."

For his part, Mark is equally aware of God's transforming—and ongoing—work in his life, and he credits his parents' steadfast love with helping draw him to Christ, even when he didn't want to receive it. "I laughed when my mom mailed me all of those Christian CDs," he says, "and I threw them away. I didn't like all their rules or the consequences I had to face. But through it all, I knew my parents loved me and that they were always praying."

Let's love our kids too. And let's never stop praying—no matter how far our teens wander or how long it takes to bring them back.

Lord, make them men—and women—of God.

Prayers You Can Use

Heavenly Father . . .

Tune _____'s ears to hear your voice so that, as Samuel did when he was a boy, they will invite you to speak and then listen to your words. *1 Samuel 3:9–10*

Allow _____ to be rooted and established in love. Give them power to grasp how wide and long and high and deep is the love of Christ. *Ephesians 3:17–18*

Cause _____ to trust you and never be shaken. *Psalm 125:1*

May _____'s faith rest not in the wisdom of human beings but in the power of God. *1 Corinthians 2:5*

Give _____ an undivided heart and a new spirit. Replace their heart of stone with a heart of flesh so that they will follow you and keep your laws. Let them know they belong to you. *Ezekiel 11:19–20*

Remove the veil from _____'s eyes so that they can see the light of the gospel. Shine your light in their heart to give them the light of the knowledge of your glory displayed in Christ. *2 Corinthians 4:3–6*

Prompt _____ to confess that Jesus is Lord. Let them believe in their heart that you have raised Jesus from the dead; may they call on your name and be saved. *Romans 10:9, 13*

Protect _____ so that they will not waver in unbelief. Strengthen their faith and cause them to give glory to God.

Romans 4:20-21

Satan wants to sift _____ like wheat, but don't let their faith fail. When they turn back to you, equip them to strengthen others.

Luke 22:31-32

Draw _____ to you. May your Holy Spirit give them life.

John 6:44, 63

Put people in _____'s life who will gently instruct them. Grant them repentance leading to a knowledge of the truth so that they will come to their senses and escape the devil's trap.

2 Timothy 2:25-26

Open _____'s eyes and turn them from darkness to light, and from the power of Satan to God, so that they may receive forgiveness of sins and a place among those who are sanctified by faith in Christ.

Acts 26:18

Grant _____ your peace. Breathe on them, that they might receive your Holy Spirit.

John 20:21-22

Bring _____ back to faith. Let our mouths be filled with laughter, and our tongues with songs of joy. Let our friends and neighbors know that you have done great things for our family.

Psalm 126:1-2

Chapter 2

Praying for Good Friends

Two people are better off than one, for they can help each other succeed. If one person falls, the other can reach out and help . . . A person standing alone can be attacked and defeated, but two can stand back-to-back and conquer.

Ecclesiastes 4:9–10, 12 NLT

When Robbie was about six or seven years old, I tiptoed into his room late one night to give him a kiss. I was surprised—and concerned—to find him awake. He was sobbing silently, the tears streaming down his sweet little cheeks.

"What is it?" I asked, feeling his forehead to see if he had a fever. "What's the matter?"

"It's just so sad to think about you having to eat lunch all alone every day at school," he said. "I feel so sorry for you."

I couldn't believe it. Sometime earlier—I couldn't even remember when—I had told my kids about my experience in middle school. To say I was not one of the popular kids would be putting it gently; truth be told, my only real friend had moved away the summer before, and I spent almost all of my eighth-grade year scanning the hallways for someone—anyone—who would meet my eyes and return my hopeful greeting. I didn't get many takers, and more often than not, I worked my way through the lunch line and tried to find a spot to sit down where I wouldn't be in anyone's way. There were plenty of days when I ate my lunch alone.

I'm not sure if there's any connection, but I also carried a big brown leather purse engraved with the words "Jesus is Lord." All the cool girls had brown leather purses, and I had begged my parents to get me one too. How was I supposed to know that they got a discount at the Christian bookstore? The other girls' purses were small and delicate—but they could afford to be, since theirs didn't bear any messages or engravings, other than a few dainty flowers.

Another unique feature of my bag was that it came with an imposing padlock—apparently, I suppose, to discourage those who didn't fully believe that Jesus is Lord from stealing my stuff. Looking back, I can't believe I carried that purse to school every day, but I did. Somewhere along the line, I had memorized the verse where Jesus says, "If anyone is ashamed of me . . . the Son of Man will be ashamed of them when he comes in his Father's glory with the holy angels"[1]—and I guess I wasn't taking any chances.

I may not have had many friends at school—and certainly none who would have joined me in professing Christ's lordship—but during the summer months, everything changed. Each year, we attended a Christian family camp, where I hung out with a diverse and eclectic group of teens from several states. They all loved the Lord, and the weeks we spent at the camp, along with the weekends during the school year when we visited each other by hopping on trains and buses, were the highlight of my middle school years. In an era before things like smartphones and social media, my camp friends and I stayed in touch by—and my kids think I'm making this up—writing letters to each other pretty much every day.[2]

I suppose my life would have gone on like that forever—spending my allowance on postage stamps and checking the mailbox when I got home from school—except that my parents started praying. They asked God to send me a Christian friend and fervently hoped that a Bible-believing family would move to town. But God had better plans. Unbeknownst to my folks, on the very day they started praying, one of the local churches began planning an evangelistic event that wound up transforming our community—teens included. Suddenly there were a whole slew of kids who wanted to get to know Jesus and who—miracle of miracles—wanted to eat lunch with *me*. It was like a Disney movie, only better!

PRAYER PRINCIPLE

Don't be surprised if God works in a way you didn't see coming. Our job is to ask; God's job is to answer.

My friend Isabelle would appreciate that story. Like my folks, she desperately wanted the Lord to bring a godly friend into her teen's life . . .

ॐ ॐ ॐ

"Why don't you invite some kids over tonight?" Isabelle offered, as her sixteen-year-old son Brian helped her unload the groceries from her car. "I bought a bunch of soft drinks, and we could order a pizza."

"Aw, Mom, nobody wants to do that."

"What do you mean? Why wouldn't your friends want to come over?"

"Nobody wants to be where they know the parents are watching," Brian replied. "Plus, all the kids know that you and Dad don't allow any drinking. Thanks anyway, but I'll pass on the party."

Isabelle sighed, hating the fact that her kids were growing up in a culture where such things as drinking and sex were considered a normal part of adolescent life. She and her husband, Craig, had been very clear about their expectations for Brian's conduct—and for the most part, he had lived up to them. Now that Brian was preparing to enter his junior year in high school, however, the temptations seemed greater than ever. In addition to alcohol and girlfriends, Isabelle found herself concerned about even simple things such as unkind words and inappropriate music and movies. "Whatever Brian does," she often prayed, using the words of Colossians 3:23, "let him work at it with all his heart, as working for you, Lord, and not to please people."

Being a people-pleaser, Isabelle knew, was yet another temptation for her son. Like most teens, he valued the friendship and opinions of his peers, and on more than one occasion, Isabelle found herself having to—as she puts it—"put myself in the way" to prevent Brian from making too many mistakes. Sometimes the boundaries Isabelle set meant that Brian was left out of parties and other social events—and during those times, she knew that her son felt the loneliness keenly. She prayed that God would send just one friend into his life—just one!—who would share his faith and hold him accountable in terms of doing things that would please the Lord. So far, though, Isabelle didn't see anyone on the horizon who fit that description.

Instead, her radar screen was filled with kids like Jarred, a fellow who had put himself on the "one to watch" list when the boys were relatively young. Jarred's older brothers had exposed him to movies, computer games, and internet sites that Isabelle did not approve of, and when he began to share his discoveries with Brian, she drew the line. "Jarred can come to our house anytime you like," she said to Brian, "but you are no longer allowed to go over there."

As the boys grew, Jarred began experimenting with sex, drinking, and drugs. By the time they hit high school, he had earned a fairly tarnished reputation among the school's faculty and on the parental grapevine. Even Jarred's standing among his peers—kids who had once looked to him as a leader—had begun to fade. Brian understood why his mom had wanted him to put some distance between himself and Jarred, so it didn't make much sense when he saw her hug him after a football game.

"Do you *like* Jarred?" Brian asked later that night.

"Of course!" Isabelle responded. "You guys have been friends since you were little kids. You've played sports together forever, and now you're on the same football team! How could I *not* like Jarred?"

"But, Mom," Brian persisted, "I don't get it. Sometimes you seem so judgmental—like when you won't let me spend the night at Jarred's house—and sometimes you seem so cool."

"Brian," Isabelle said slowly, "this may be hard to understand, but when your friends look at me, I want them to see Jesus and his love, not just some judgmental, overprotective parent. I know that Jarred has made some pretty big mistakes—and that's why I don't let you do everything he and some of the other kids do—but the bottom line is that I want to love your friends and encourage them, and I'm asking God to help me do that."

Loving and encouraging Brian's friends was the right thing to do—Isabelle had no doubt about that. The thing she sometimes questioned, though, was whether it was wise for her to prevent Brian from doing the things he wanted to do. After all, he would be in college in two years. If she kept putting herself in the way of potentially bad friendships and decisions, would he be prepared for the choices he would have to make when he was on his own? She needed God's wisdom to know when to hold her son back and when to let him go.

Isabelle knew the year ahead would be a critical one. Brian would be stepping onto the football field as the team's starting quarterback—a position that afforded him an unprecedented opportunity for influence. Kids who once looked to Jarred to call the shots were starting to look to Brian for leadership. It was a subtle shift, but one that did not go unnoticed in Isabelle's eyes. Time—and God—certainly had a way of turning things around.

When one of the football coaches approached Brian about starting a Fellowship of Christian Athletes group for his teammates, Isabelle sensed that God was doing something that went beyond her expectations.[3] She had prayed that God would send a Christian friend to help him stand strong; now it looked as though God could be planning to use Brian to strengthen and encourage other kids. Eager to align her prayers with God's purposes, Isabelle broadened the scope of her request. "Let Brian live wisely among those who are not Christians," she prayed, using the words of Colossians 4:5, "and help him to make the most of every opportunity."

Like most of the stories in this book, Brian's is still being written. Isabelle has seen God's hand at work—both in protecting her son from negative influences and in elevating him to a position of leadership among his peers—and she is grateful. She still wants godly friends to surround her son (what praying parent wouldn't?) but she is learning to let God do things his way, and in his timing.

Poised for Prayer

Friends are the greatest influence on our teens today—greater than the media or family life—and a kid's desire to be accepted, to belong to a "group," will inform their behavior and their choices more than anything else. "Walk with the wise and become wise," Scripture says, "associate with fools and get in trouble."[4]

That admonition was never far from my friend Cindy's mind as she raised her teens, and she prayed that they would be surrounded by "people of good influence." She knew—and fully believed—verses like 1 Corinthians 15:33 ("Bad company corrupts good character"), but as she looked across the landscape of her kids' lives, she didn't see all that many people who fell into the "good company" category. "Slim pickings" was how she put it. Not knowing what else to do, she asked God to put a hedge of protection around her kids as they spent time with their peers and equip them to *be* people of good influence.[5]

Cindy's daughter got married not long ago. Words can't describe the joy, the life, the *vibrancy* that this young woman radiated—and not just the bride but the whole pack of bridesmaids and groomsmen and the entourage of friends who crowded onto the dance floor. "Slim pickings" had turned into a bountiful harvest—almost every one of these young people had professed faith in Christ, and it showed! God had answered Cindy's prayers with an abundance that exceeded her wildest dreams.

I wish I could say that this sort of answer to prayer always happens. Sadly, it doesn't. As one of my youth group leader friends put it, "It's much easier to pull someone off a chair than to pull them up onto it." Bad company really does corrupt good character, more than the other way around.

So what can we do?

We can do like Cindy did, and ask God to put a hedge around our teens. We can pay attention to our kids' social lives—and pray them out of any destructive friendships. And more than anything else, we can point them toward friendship with Jesus—the one who laid down his life, the one who calls them his friends, and the one who will never forsake them.[6]

PRAYER PRINCIPLE

Teen friends may come and go, but the
Lord will never abandon your child.

As we pray for our teens, let's remind them of God's immeasurable love—and his absolute faithfulness—as often as we can. Let's also encourage them to look for ways to *give* love and acceptance to their peers—being willing to put others' needs and interests ahead of their own—even though they may be more inclined to focus on *receiving* it. It may look like slim pickings on your teen's social horizon right now, but don't despair. Instead, keep praying, remembering Paul's charge in Galatians 6:9: "Let us not become weary in doing good, for at the proper time we will reap a harvest if we do not give up."

Prayers You Can Use

Heavenly Father . . .

Surround _____ with good friends—those who will sharpen
them as iron sharpens iron.   *Proverbs 27:17*

Prompt _____ to pursue faith and love and peace, and let
them enjoy the companionship of those who call on you out of a
pure heart.   *2 Timothy 2:22*

Don't allow _____ to follow the crowd in doing wrong.
                                                               Exodus 23:2

You promise to be a friend to those who fear you. Be _____ 's
friend, and teach them your covenant. May _____ keep their
eyes always on you and be rescued from any trap.
                                                               Psalm 25:14–15 NLT

Don't let _____ exclude peers or participate in gossip, since
a perverse person stirs up dissension, and a gossip separates
close friends.   *Proverbs 16:28*

Show _____ how to love others with the same self-sacrificing
love you have shown. Make them willing to lay down all they have
for their friends. Prompt _____ to obey you and let them find
security in the fact that you confide in them and have chosen
them as your friend.   *John 15:12–15*

Use _____ to spread the fragrance of the knowledge of you. Let them be the aroma of the knowledge of Christ everywhere.

2 Corinthians 2:15–16

Teach _____ how to show love even to their enemies and to pray for kids who may reject or persecute them. Remind them that even pagans are kind to their own people, but that, as a child of God, they are called to love everyone.

Matthew 5:44–47

Don't let _____ pay back evil for evil, but cause them to focus on forgiveness, which breaks down walls between friends and restores relationships.   *Genesis 50:14–21*

Let _____ walk in the light of your presence and enjoy fellowship with other teens who love you.   *1 John 1:7*

When _____ wrestles with loneliness or rejection, remind them of your promise: though the mountains be shaken and the hills be removed, your unfailing love will never be shaken and your covenant of peace will not be removed.   *Isaiah 54:10*

When _____ feels like friends have rejected or deserted them, remind them that you are a friend who sticks closer than anyone.   *Proverbs 18:24*

Equip _____ to speak the truth to their friends in love, supporting them and building them up by all they say and do.

Ephesians 4:15–16

May _____ walk with the wise and become wise, since a companion of fools gets in trouble and bad company corrupts good character.

Proverbs 13:20 NLT; 1 Corinthians 15:33

Send _____ a friend who will be a partner in spreading the good news about Jesus Christ. Let them pray for one another, giving joyful thanks to you for the gift of their friendship.

Philippians 1:3–5

Chapter 3

Praying for Connection to a Church Community

Let us consider how we may spur one another on toward love and good deeds, not giving up meeting together, as some are in the habit of doing, but encouraging one another—and all the more as you see the Day approaching.

Hebrews 10:24–25

Once upon a time, I led a Bible study for middle school girls. Somewhere along the line, the youth leaders at our church wisely decided that the girls would enjoy having an older teen in the mix so it wasn't just them and an "old lady" getting together every week. They partnered me with a beautiful redhead named Cally, a high school junior who knew how to do pretty much everything—from making beaded bracelets out of lengths of twine to dishing out godly advice on boys, schoolwork, sports, fashion, and a host of other life-and-death teen concerns.

Like the girls, I quickly fell in love with Cally—but not just because she seemed so effortlessly cool and accomplished. I loved her heart. Not only was Cally eager to invest in the lives of a group of middle school girls, but her passion for God and for sharing his love had taken her to places most teens would never put on their bucket list: she had traveled to Thailand do to relief work after a devastating tsunami, to China to teach English classes, and to the Dominican Republic to help stage a Vacation Bible School.

More remarkable than these things, though, was Cally's commitment to church. The global travel offered adventure; getting up early on a Sunday morning to sit in a hard pew in a very traditional sanctuary was not, I thought, something that would make a teen's toes tingle. And yet Cally was there every week, both on Sunday morning and at the Sunday night youth group. With a heavy academic load and a schedule bursting with school sports, student government, and even a role in the high school musical, how had she managed to keep church involvement at the top of her priority list? Why was she there?

"My parents took us to church when we were young, and we didn't question it," Cally told me. "By the time we hit the teen years—when we were more apt to question things—the idea of *not* going to church just wasn't an option.

"But even more than that," Cally added, "I think I got involved in church after one of the youth leaders, Sara, reached out to me and invested her time in my life. Church groups can sometimes be sort of cliquey, and having a friend or someone to welcome you can make all the difference."

PRAYER PRINCIPLE

Having a friend can make all the difference. Ask God to send someone to welcome your teen to church.

Like Cally, Eric was a bright student with an easygoing manner, a loving family, and plenty of extracurricular activities to be involved in. Unlike Cally, though, he had little interest in going to church, and even less in getting involved in any sort of youth group or mission work. In his mind, the teens at church were a bunch of goofballs, and he wanted no part of their antics. Eric's mother, Jackie, found herself wondering where to turn for help ...

ॐ ॐ ॐ

"You can't make me go back! I hate you!"

Jackie flinched at her son's words. Eric had always been a kind and courteous kid, and she had never heard him lash out at her—or anyone else—with such venom. Even so, she knew he didn't really hate her; he was just mad because she was making him go to youth group.

Was this one of those battles worth fighting? Jackie wasn't sure. Reflecting on her own upbringing—she had been dropped off at the church door every week by parents who weren't interested in anything "religious" but who figured that church would be a good thing for their daughter—Jackie had resolved that once she was married and had children, they would go to church *as a family*.

The first hurdle had been Jackie's husband, Peter. A sporadic churchgoer, it wasn't until he realized the influence his behavior had on his teen son—who argued that if Dad wasn't going to church, he shouldn't have to go either—that Peter began to show up on Sunday mornings. He didn't plan to *enjoy* church; he simply went to please his wife and set an example for his son. Somewhat to his surprise, however, he found himself hooked.

Eric, though, was another story. He didn't like church; he tolerated it because he had to. Jackie had been inspired by her Bible study teacher, a woman with five children who claimed that keeping the fourth commandment—remembering the Sabbath day—was one of the secrets of her family's love for each other and for the Lord. Citing verses like Isaiah 58:13–14 (which promise joy and rewards to those who honor the Sabbath), the Bible study teacher said that, whether they wanted to or not, her kids knew they had to be in church on Sunday. Jackie figured that if this woman could get *five* teens to church—and if it really had made a difference in their lives—then surely she could wrangle *one* teen into the pew.

And so she and Peter and Eric began attending church together as a family, and Jackie thanked God for the realization of her childhood dream. It wasn't long before she caught wind of the neat things taking place in the church's large and vibrant youth group. The Sunday night gatherings were filled with singing, skits, inspirational talks, and a ton of laughter. Jackie knew she was pushing it, but she decided to broach the subject with Eric.

It didn't go over well.

"What?" he said. "Now you want me to go to church in the morning *and* at night? Mom, I know what the kids at that youth group do. They do stupid stuff like throw donuts at each other. They are loud and wild—definitely not my kind of people."

"But you don't even *know* those kids!" Jackie protested.

"Exactly!" Eric agreed. "So why would I want to hang out with them?"

Undaunted, Jackie turned to the youth group leader for advice.

"Bring him for four consecutive Sundays," the man advised.

"If he gets to know some of the other kids and sees what a good time we have, he will want to come back."

That sounded good, but after the first week—and Eric's uncharacteristically heated reaction—Jackie lost her resolve. She knew better than to take his "I hate you" comment personally, but she didn't want to start a war with her son over youth group. After all, Eric was going to church every Sunday. Jackie decided to be content with that.

And she decided to pray.

As much as she hated to admit it, Jackie knew she was probably not in the best position to influence the thoughts and attitudes of her teen son. Like most teens, Eric tended to view his friends' advice as far more valid and noteworthy than his parents' counsel. "Lord," Jackie prayed, "please open a door into Eric's heart through your Holy Spirit. Bring a friend into his life who will invite him to church. Draw him closer to you."

Whether Jackie knew it or not, her prayers were a potent combination of Scripture. Colossians 4:3 speaks to the need for an open door for God's word. Proverbs 17:17 talks about the power of faithful, loving friends. And John 6:44 points to the fact that no one comes to Jesus unless the Father draws him. It wasn't long before God's answers began to take shape—starting with his provision of a friend.

Heather was a gregarious and fun-loving girl who liked nothing more than making friends and introducing them to Jesus. Captivated as he was by her enthusiasm and joy, Eric failed to consider the fact that Heather might turn out to be one of those wild donut-throwers, and when she invited him to join her at youth group, he quickly said yes.

Heather introduced Eric to other kids at church and invited

him to join the group at an overnight camp. When he asked permission to go, Jackie played it cool. She wanted to jump up and down; instead, she calmly filled out the camp forms. And she continued to pray.

At the camp, Eric surrendered his life to the Lord.

That was three years ago. Today, as Jackie tells it, the transformation in her son could not be more amazing. Not only has he participated in summer mission projects and other youth group events, but Eric has followed Heather's lead in bringing other kids to church. Stuff that once looked corny or boring is actually, Eric admits, a whole lot of fun.

"It's beyond anything I could have ever asked for," Jackie says. "I trusted God to work in Eric's life, and he has answered my prayers a hundred times beyond anything I could have ever imagined."

Looking back, Jackie acknowledges it would have been far easier to let Eric—and, for that matter, her husband, Peter—stay home on Sundays than to prod him on toward church. But she believes that her job description as a mother and wife includes prodding—as well as a whole lot of praying and persevering. Jackie didn't know whether it would take weeks or months or years to bring that vision to reality; what she did know was that getting her son connected to church and to other believers was something that really mattered.

"It definitely took a willingness to hang in there, to prod, and to pray," Jackie says. "But it was worth it."

Poised for Prayer

One of the things I appreciated most about Jackie's story is that she desperately wanted her son to be involved in church, but she didn't sit in her pew comparing herself to other mothers or wondering why Eric couldn't be more like the youth group kids. She didn't worry about what she might have done *wrong*; rather, she focused on what she could do that was *right*—seeking advice from the youth pastor, keeping the lines of communication open with her son, and, most important of all, steadfastly taking her concerns to the only One who could do anything about them.

I believe that as God looked at Jackie—and as he looks at us as we persevere in prayer—his perspective encompasses far more than anything our human eyes could ever perceive. You may *feel* like a battle-weary soldier, but God sees you as a faithful warrior. You may *think* that nothing is changing, but God hears your prayers. He calls into being things that are not, and he promises to finish the good work that he has already begun.[1]

PRAYER PRINCIPLE

God doesn't call parents to be successful;
he calls us to be faithful.

Whether you are waging a "prayer battle" to get your teen to church or wrestling over some other issue, consider the perspective shared by Mother Teresa. Surrounded by the overwhelming tide of poverty and problems that threatened her Calcutta ministry, she refused to give in to defeat or despair. "God doesn't call me to be successful," she said. "He calls me to be faithful."

Moms and Dads, that's God's call to us too. We may want to tidy our teens' lives with one broad wave of a magic wand, but that's not God's way. God works in the midst of people and problems—not independently of them. And his charge to us, as we wait on him to bring about all that he has promised, is that we should be "joyful in hope, patient in affliction, faithful in prayer."[2]

Precious Lord, make us faithful in prayer.

Prayers You Can Use

Heavenly Father . . .

As we pray for _____'s involvement in church, help us hold tightly to hope, knowing that you are faithful. Let us consider how we can spur them on toward love and good deeds.

Hebrews 10:23–24

Don't let _____ give up meeting together with other believers, even if some of their friends quit going to church, but show them how they can love and encourage others.

Hebrews 10:25

Let _____ be like King David, rejoicing with those who say, "Let us go to the house of the Lord." *Psalm 122:1*

Remind _____ of your promise that where two or three come together in your name, you are there with them.

Matthew 18:20

Cause _____ to be devoted to godly teaching and to fellowship. May they be prayerful, generous, and willing to share. Give them favor with other teens so that the group of believers will grow. *Acts 2:42–47*

Teach _____ to remember the Sabbath day and keep it holy.

Exodus 20:8

Help our family to understand what it means to call the Sabbath a delight and to make it an honorable day. Show us how to find joy in you rather than in doing whatever we please.

Isaiah 58:13-14

Equip our church leaders to preach your word with great patience and careful instruction so that when _____ encounters those who reject sound doctrine in favor of teachers who tell them whatever they want to hear, they can stand firm and spot the difference between truth and myths. *2 Timothy 4:2-4*

As _____ hears your word taught in church, may they receive the message with eagerness and examine the Scriptures every day to see if the teaching is true. *Acts 17:11*

Make _____ like Lydia, who listened to the apostles teach on the Sabbath. Open _____'s heart so that they will respond to your message and want to be with other believers.

Acts 16:13-14

Let _____ enjoy the company of people who are "salty"— those who create a thirst for Jesus. Help _____ and the other teens in our church live at peace with each other.

Mark 9:50

Give _____ the same Spirit that Jesus had as a young man. Let them be an eager listener and an active participant at church, and bless them with wisdom and understanding.

Luke 2:46-47

Draw _____ to you and give them friends in church who will make them sharp. *John 6:44; Proverbs 27:17*

May _____ seek and desire only one thing: to dwell in your house and gaze on your beauty, seeking you in your temple.

Psalm 27:4

Chapter 4

Praying for Dating Relationships

Above all else, guard your heart,
for everything you do flows from it.
Proverbs 4:23

When I first sat down to work on this chapter, I grabbed a copy of *Praying the Scriptures for Your Children* from my bookshelf. Not wanting to repeat myself, I was eager to see what I had written about dating relationships in the earlier book. Much to my shock and chagrin, I found that I hadn't written anything. Not even a paragraph! There's a chapter on praying for your child's friendships and another one about marriage—but what about all those in-between years, the ones where your son's hormones are raging and your daughter—okay, *my* daughter—brings home a guy whose idea of "meet the family" fashion is a shirt with a cussword on it? *What was I thinking*, neglecting an entire prayer season like that?

Looking back, I realized that Hillary—the oldest of our four children—had just celebrated her tenth birthday when I turned in the first *Praying the Scriptures* manuscript. At a time when we spent most nights memorizing math facts and tucked the children into bed as soon as the sun went down, things like dating and curfews weren't even on my radar screen. I remember working on an article about courtship for *Focus on the Family* magazine. Courtship, an alternative to traditional dating, allows a guy who is serious about a girl to spend time "courting" her (in the presence of family members or trusted friends), so he can determine whether she is "the one" (and so she and her family can eyeball him at the same time). I found the subject intriguing and—since Hillary had a third-grade diorama project on *Stuart Little* due the same week—entirely forgettable. After all, we had *years* to go before we had to figure out all that boyfriend-girlfriend stuff.

Fast-forward to our kids' teen years. Robbie and I put some boundaries in place—only to be told we were "the strictest parents in the whole school." I knew better than to fall for that line, but I also knew we needed some help. I began reaching out to older friends—parents who had made it through the angst-filled season of adolescent romance and whose children went on to the marriage aisle with their purity—and their hearts—intact.

"We were committed to the idea of courtship, so our kids didn't date," one mother told me. "It wasn't easy. I remember standing next to the vegetables in our grocery store while a woman I knew screamed at me, telling me we were crazy and that everyone was talking about how weird we were."

"We allowed our kids to date, but we had some rules," another friend confided. "One was that they couldn't be at anyone's house if the parents weren't home. One time, my husband and I dropped our daughter off at a boy's house, and then, when we noticed there were no cars in the driveway, we went back and rang the doorbell. The fellow assured us his folks would be 'right back.' We waited—somewhat to our daughter's mortification—but they never showed up. The boy had lied to our daughter, knowing she would never have come over had she known that his parents were gone."

"When my children were teens," a single mom said, "they hung out a lot in groups. When their friends began pairing off, I prayed for a hedge of protection to be put around their emotions so they would not be drawn to anyone God didn't want them to be with. I remember not liking my son's girlfriend very much when he first brought her home. By the time they got engaged, however, I found myself grateful that God had done the picking and not me—she is absolutely perfect for my son."

Suffice it to say that within the realm of Christian parenting there is a *huge* spectrum of perspectives, practices, and even prayers about dating. I have a friend who is always looking for a set of rules or a formula for godly living—"Just tell me how to do it, God, and I will," she says—and I'm afraid she is going to hate this chapter. The more parents I talk with, the more convinced I am that teen dating is one of those areas where, as soon as you think you have a workable system, God throws you a curveball.

My friend Teri, for example, is a homeschooling former missionary who has done pretty much everything "right." She'd be lightning-quick to counter that claim, but from where I sit, her kids look fairly fantastic. They are athletic, smart, respectful, kind, and—best of all—absolutely in love with Jesus. But when her oldest daughter developed more than a passing interest in a boy she had met at church, Teri and her husband, Bart, knew it was a relationship that could rock their world . . .

∂∿ ∂∿ ∂∿

> "But, Mom, I really like him! Justin is an amaz-
> ing guy. You and Daddy *have* to let me go out
> with him—please!"

Teri listened to Wendy's impassioned plea and wondered if she could be dreaming. If she had the right boy—and she knew she did—she couldn't see any way her daughter could be attracted to him. Wendy was a rule follower, a straight-A student, and a talented and hardworking athlete. Justin was an overweight pot-head who had recently been kicked out of school.

Well, okay, maybe he wasn't technically a pothead. But Justin *had* smoked the stuff—everyone knew it—and that, coupled with a long history of disrespect for teachers and a blowout night of binge drinking, had resulted in his expulsion from the Christian school that Teri and Bart's older children attended. Teri was as willing to extend grace as the next person, but as she reflected on the chaos that Justin had caused in the classes he shared with Wendy's sister, Samantha, she had to admit she didn't blame the school for asking him to leave. No doubt about it—the boy was Trouble, with a capital *T*.

The irony of it all, Teri realized, was that Wendy hadn't even noticed Justin at school. They had kindled a friendship on a mis-sion trip sponsored by their church. A mission trip! How did a kid like Justin even get to *go* on a mission trip?

If that was God's way of being funny, Teri wasn't laughing.

Truth be told, Teri knew why Justin had been part of the mission team. The expulsion had served as a wake-up call of sorts, and Justin had recommitted his life to the Lord. He began showing up at church and youth group events, and—over the protests of a few adults in the church who saw him as a dangerous influence on their teens—one of the youth directors had accepted his application for the team. "He's ready," the director had said, putting an end to the discussion.

With his long hair, baggy clothes, and six-foot-seven-inch-anything-but-lanky frame, Justin looked, Teri thought, more ready to serve time than he did to serve God. When she and Bart had taught Wendy to pay more attention to someone's heart than to his outward appearance, Teri never dreamed her daughter would take them *that* seriously.

"Okay," she found herself saying in response to Wendy's request. "You and Justin can spend time together. But you can't be alone. You can see him at youth group, or if a group of kids goes out to lunch after church."

Wondering how long the attraction would last, Teri and Bart decided to pull their youth pastor into the discussion. "We want you to know what's going on between Wendy and Justin," they confided. "We're not very comfortable with their relationship, and we'd be grateful if you could keep an eye on them while they're at church."

"All right," the pastor said, "but there's something you should know. When we were in the Dominican Republic, nobody—and I mean nobody—worked harder or demonstrated as much integrity as Justin."

Somewhat mollified, Teri and Bart kept any further reservations to themselves, confident that Wendy would lose interest in Justin soon enough. If nothing else, the fact that college was just around the corner would shake things loose. Wendy was a rising senior with the grades and other achievements she needed to get into a Top-25 school, and she had expressed interest in a string of colleges dotting the Eastern Seaboard.

A couple of months passed, and Wendy's attachment to Justin looked stronger than ever. The only thing that had changed, it seemed, were the geographic boundaries she put on her college search. "I'm thinking of going someplace closer to home, maybe an hour or so away," she said—leaving no doubt about her plans to put as little distance as possible between herself and her man.

Things finally came to a head one afternoon when Teri and Wendy were home alone. "Can Justin and I go out for dinner tonight?" Wendy asked.

"Sure—as long as you're with a group of kids," Teri said, reciting the guidelines she and Bart had placed on the time the couple spent together.

"Mom!" Wendy cried. "Why are you and Daddy making this so hard? If I were dating some other guy from church—somebody who could talk the talk and who looked the look—it wouldn't be any problem for us to be together. You're not being fair!"

"Wendy," Teri said, struggling to keep the emotion out of her voice, "it all has to do with Justin's track record. I know he seems like a great guy to you, but it's only been a couple of months since he was making some pretty bad choices. You are our daughter, and we love you. We just need you to be careful."

"I'll be in college next year!" Wendy wailed. "You have to start giving me my freedom!"

"I know, and we will."

"When?" Wendy demanded angrily. "How much longer are you and Daddy going to try to keep us apart?"

"I can't give you an answer on that right now," Teri sighed. "We just need you to trust us." Being a natural peacemaker, she hated the way the conversation was going. Teri decided to go downstairs before saying something she might regret.

"Lord," she prayed, "you are the only one who can work this out. Bart and I believe we need to stand firm on this one. I thought I could make Wendy see that we're just trying to love and protect her, but I can't. We need you, Lord."

An hour later, Teri went back upstairs. Tentatively, she opened Wendy's bedroom door, expecting a stony reception. Instead, Wendy jumped up and bounded across the room.

"You're not going to believe what happened!" Wendy said, wrapping her arms around her mother.

"Tell me!" Teri gasped.

"After you left my room, I called Justin. He said I had really messed up, and that it was my job to respect you and Daddy. I hung up the phone and decided to read my Bible and pray. I felt like God was telling me I had a choice to make. I could trust him and obey you—or not. I decided I should obey you."

"You did?" Teri could hardly believe her ears.

"Yes—but Mom, that's not the best part. When we were arguing earlier, I thought my life was *over*. But once I made the decision to obey you, I found myself just filled up with joy. It's amazing!"

Yes, Teri agreed, it was amazing. *God* was amazing. All that Teri had been hoping—praying—for was a little peace between herself and her strong-willed daughter, and God had done so much more. The transformation reminded her of Jesus' promise: "When you obey my commandments . . . you will be filled with my joy. Yes, your joy will overflow!"[1]

PRAYER PRINCIPLE

When you don't see eye to eye with your
teen about a dating relationship, ask
God to give you his perspective.

Not only had God brought peace and joy into their home, but, Teri realized, he had answered another prayer. She and Bart had been asking God to help Wendy and Justin sharpen one another, according to Proverbs 27:17. Embarrassed as she was to admit it, Teri acknowledged that she had been counting on Wendy to "sharpen" Justin's spiritual life—but she hadn't really expected the prayer to work in reverse.

God had used Justin—with his checkered past and his grungy-looking present—to show them a little slice of his glory.

Poised for Prayer

I mentioned earlier that perspectives and practices on teen dating vary widely among families. Maybe that's because the Bible doesn't give a whole lot of commands or specific information on the subject. There are plenty of principles and proverbs—things like "guard your heart" and "do not be yoked together with unbelievers"[2]—but rarely do we find hard-and-fast rules like, "Be home by eleven o'clock."

That being said, the Bible does offer relevant verses that dovetail neatly with commonsense parenting wisdom. For example:

- Make sure your teen has a predetermined escape plan in case they need to get out of an uncomfortable or potentially dangerous situation. As 2 Timothy 2:22 puts it, our kids need to "flee the evil desires of youth."

- Remind your teen—and your teen's date—of the importance of honor. Romans 12:10 reads, "Be devoted to one another in love. Honor one another above yourselves." Honoring someone means putting their needs ahead of your own, demonstrating respect, and—in a nutshell—treating the other person the way you hope some guy or girl is treating your future spouse.

- Set boundaries for things like physical intimacy, and be specific. There's a lot more to maintaining pure hearts, minds, and bodies than just not having sex. Song of Songs 2:7 cautions against prematurely arousing or awakening feelings of love, and 1 Thessalonians 4:3–5 is even more blunt: "It is God's will that . . . each of you should learn to control your own body in a way that is holy and honorable, not in passionate lust like the pagans, who do not know God."

- Encourage group dating so as to avoid both temptation and rumor. The KJV's rendering of 1 Thessalonians 5:22 exhorts us to avoid even the *"appearance* of evil"—and if we're going to start putting things in italics, I may as well throw in Ephesians 5:3: "Among you there must not be even a *hint* of sexual immorality."

- Evaluate dating relationships based on how time spent together affects teens' attitudes and behavior. What we want to see is the fulfillment of verses such as Hebrews 10:24: "Let us consider how we may spur one another on toward love and good deeds." Young people may be too emotionally involved with one another to be objective;

encourage your teens to ask their friends what they think. "Are we good together? Do you like who I am when I'm with this person?"

PRAYER PRINCIPLE

Ask God to connect your teen with someone who makes them better, someone who spurs them on toward love and good deeds.

These are, of course, just a handful of practical pointers; I'm sure that, if we put our parenting heads together, we could come up with a whole book full of similar nuggets. At the end of the day, though, even my formula-loving friend would agree that what we really want isn't a set of pointers or rules. What we want—for ourselves and for our teens—is a *relationship*: a hope-infusing, wisdom-giving, life-changing relationship with Jesus himself. As we pray for our kids, asking for things such as wisdom and protection in their dating relationships, let's ask God to take hold of their hearts, directing them, as Scripture puts it, like "a stream of water."[3]

Let's ask God to direct our teens' hearts toward him.

Prayers You Can Use

Heavenly Father . . .

Let _____ be drawn to relationships that will sharpen them spiritually and mentally and allow them to bring out the best in others.   *Proverbs 27:17*

Guard _____'s heart, since everything flows from that.
                                                    Proverbs 4:23

Remind _____ of your counsel not to be "yoked together" with those who do not know you. Let them take the question "What does a believer have in common with an unbeliever?" seriously as they think about romantic relationships.
                                              2 Corinthians 6:14–15

Set a hedge of protection around _____, that they may be protected from harm and find their hearts drawn only to people you choose.   *Job 1:10*

Let _____'s love be sincere. Cause them to hate what is evil and to cling to what is good. Let them be devoted to others in love, honoring dating partners and/or potential spouses above themselves.   *Romans 12:9–10*

When _____ has to choose between obedience to you and going their own way, prompt them to choose obedience and thereby open the door to overflowing joy.   *John 15:10–11*

As _____ considers romantic relationships, let them submit to your authority so that your peace can rule in their heart, causing them to know exactly what they should say or do and whether a particular interest is pleasing to you.   *Colossians 3:15*

As _____ spends time with their peers, let them be careful and watch themselves closely so that they do not forget your commands or let them slip from their heart.

Deuteronomy 4:9

Cause _____'s love to abound more and more in knowledge and depth of insight, so that they may be able to discern what is best and may be pure and blameless until the day of Christ.

Philippians 1:9–10

Equip _____ to flee from sexual immorality, recognizing that their body is a temple of the Holy Spirit. Remind them that they belong to you and that they should honor you with their body.

1 Corinthians 6:18–20

When _____ yearns for a dating relationship, help them to stay watchful and prayerful so that they will not fall into temptation. Let them be strong and take heart as they wait on your perfect provision.   *Matthew 26:41; Psalm 27:14*

Be faithful to _____. Do not let them be tempted beyond what they can bear, but provide a way of escape so that they can endure.   *1 Corinthians 10:13 ESV*

As we establish rules and boundaries for dating in our home, give us wisdom and knowledge, so that we may properly lead our teens, for they are precious in your sight, and they belong to you.

2 Chronicles 1:10

In _____'s dating relationships, may they acknowledge you as Lord.

Philippians 2:11

Chapter 5

Praying for Your Teen's Relationship with You

Children, obey your parents in everything,
for this pleases the Lord.
Fathers, do not embitter your children,
or they will become discouraged.
Colossians 3:20-21

In the 2003 movie *Cheaper by the Dozen*, there's a scene in which actor Steve Martin (playing the dad) confronts his son "Charlie" about a missed curfew, his girlfriend, and his plans for college—none of which Charlie seems all that eager to discuss. In the end, Martin asks Charlie if there is anything else he'd like to talk about.

"Have I mentioned that I don't like you very much?" Charlie says.

"You mentioned that," Martin acknowledges.

"Then I'm good," Charlie says, with a smile on his face.

I love this scene because while it's clear that father and son love each other, it's equally obvious they are not on the same wavelength. You don't need to be a family psychologist to know that parents and teens often see things very differently—and even in families where folks truly love each other, there will be times when we might not *like* each other all that much.

We live in a culture that tends to eye the parent-teen relationship with a mixture of fear and uncertainty. When conflict happens—as it inevitably does—we often point at our teens, fingering them as the source of the problem. After all, they're the ones with the raging hormones and all the attitudes, right?

Right—and wrong. Teens have attitudes—nobody says they don't—but so do we. And before we go saddling our kids with blame, we need to turn the mirror on ourselves. In his book *Age of Opportunity*, Paul David Tripp says that the teen years are often hard for parents because "they expose the wrong thoughts and desires of our *own* hearts"—things like self-righteousness, impatience, and a desire for our kids to succeed so that *we* will look good.[1]

Ouch. No wonder our daughter Hillary says she wants to write *Praying the Scriptures for Your Parents*.

PRAYER PRINCIPLE

As you pray for your teen's attitude,
ask God to expose any wrong thoughts
and desires in your own heart.

I'm sure the experts could come up with all sorts of contributing factors for the tension that often colors the parent-teen relationship, but as I've conducted my own informal research—as in, when I talk to other moms—an issue that seems to crop up again and again is the parent's need for control. I know our teens have their own hearts to tame, but as I look at what we can do to improve the climate in our homes, being willing to "let go and let God" is certainly part of the package. Every other chapter in this book centers on our teens and the issues they face; I want to take a few pages now to turn the spotlight on us.

Leslie is a mother I know only through email. Like me, she has three girls and one boy. And also like me, she finds herself having to make what can feel like a million little decisions every day: Can I go to the concert? Can I sleep at John's house? Can I borrow the car? Can I go to Sally's party? Can I . . .?

*Un*like me, though, Leslie has learned to trust God to help her know when to hold her ground and when to let go. And in a world filled with tug-of-war issues, letting God call the shots can make all the difference . . .

∾ ∾ ∾

"That's not fair!" Sara Kay cried, a look of anguish crossing her pretty face. "It's my senior prom!"

"I realize that, honey," Leslie answered calmly. "But it's also your sister's college graduation. You went to the prom last year. This year, we're going—as a family—to be with Rebecca. Case closed."

Sara Kay stomped off, and Leslie thought she had heard the end of it. Two weeks later, though, Sara Kay skipped into the kitchen. "Riley asked me to go to prom with him!" she exclaimed.

"What did you tell him?" Leslie queried.

"I said yes, of course!"

"Sara Kay," Leslie said slowly, "you know how much we all like

Riley. But you can't go with him. In case you've forgotten, we're all going to be at Rebecca's graduation."

"But Mom," Sara Kay protested, "I talked to Rebecca and she said she doesn't mind if I go to prom."

"That's what she says now. But down the road, she might feel differently. Prom happens every year, and you've gone before. Rebecca will only graduate from college once."

"But the dance is on Saturday night. I could fly up on Sunday morning and be with the family for Rebecca's ceremony. Pleeeeease, Mom!"

"Listen, Sara Kay. As far as I'm concerned, this subject is not open to discussion. You can talk to God about it if you want, but I'm not changing my mind unless he intervenes. Now go tell Riley you can't go with him so he'll have time to ask someone else."

Sara Kay did talk to Riley—and to God. Meanwhile, Leslie found herself wondering if she had made the right decision. She had nothing against the prom, and Riley was a family friend who would certainly be a safe and courteous date—but didn't her daughter realize that a college graduation was more important than a dance? Her husband seemed open to the idea of letting Sara Kay go to the prom; was she making a mistake by insisting that the family stay together for the entire graduation weekend? "God," she prayed silently, "let me be open to whatever you want for Sara Kay."

The next few days were a whirlwind of change and activity. A neighbor—who had been wanting to attend the graduation anyway—offered to travel with Sara Kay, and they managed to find a cheap flight that would get them to the school in time for the ceremony. Another neighbor said that Sara Kay could spend the night with her after the dance. For her part, Sara Kay agreed to skip the after-prom parties and promised to be home by midnight. Leslie felt the reins of control slipping out of her fingertips, but—somewhat to her surprise—it didn't matter. She realized that God had changed her heart.

And when her cell phone rang late on prom night, it all made sense. "Mom," Sara Kay said, her voice breathless with excitement, "guess what?"

"What?"

"I was chosen as prom queen! And Riley was the king!"

Leslie thought she might drop the phone. Making her daughter miss the prom would have been one thing; making her miss being the queen—a once-in-a-lifetime event—would have been something else entirely. And God had known all along what would happen!

"God taught me a wonderful family lesson," Leslie told me later. "By trusting him and being open to his intervention, we avoided the guilt and resentment that could have cropped up had I insisted that we do things the way that made sense to me. I learned that if we seek the Lord in our family decisions, letting him reign instead of always trying to be in control all by ourselves, he will keep us from making really big mistakes."

Poised for Prayer

As a mom who does not like to give up control, I love the lessons in Leslie's story. I love that she asked the Lord to soften her heart—something she could not do on her own. I love that she taught her daughter to bring her concerns to God—thereby nourishing a prayer relationship that Sara Kay can rely on throughout her life. And I love what she said about being open to God's intervention, even when it didn't make sense to her. As God reminds us in Isaiah 55:8, his thoughts are not our thoughts, and his ways are not our ways. They are—as the NLT puts it—"far beyond anything you could imagine."

Happily for us, God took the time to make many of his thoughts clear to us through the pages of Scripture. There may not be a formula for creating the perfect parent-teen relationship, but the verses at the beginning of this chapter—Colossians 3:20–21—are a good place to start. The first part (where God tells children to obey their parents) is one of those commands that gets repeated over and over again in the Bible. God introduces the concept of filial honor in the fifth commandment—"Honor your father and your mother"—and then he repeats the charge in Leviticus, Deuteronomy, Proverbs, Matthew, Mark, Colossians, and Ephesians.[2] Not only does God take the honoring thing seriously, but he adds that when children honor and obey their parents, they will reap a "long, full life" in which "things will go well" for them.[3] When we pray that our teens will honor us, we are not being selfish or controlling; rather, we are opening the door to a lifetime of God's best!

If your kids aren't the type to be motivated by promises like a life full of blessing, you can always try the opposite approach. Point them toward helpful verses like Proverbs 30:17: "The eye that mocks a father, that scorns an aged mother, will be pecked out by the ravens of the valley, will be eaten by the vultures." Talk about your inspirational passages!

PRAYER PRINCIPLE

When we pray that our teens will honor
and obey us, we are opening the door
to a lifetime of God's blessing.

As we pray for our teens to honor us, let's not forget the second part of the Colossian charge: "Fathers [and mothers], do not embitter your children, or they will become discouraged." God wants us to teach and correct and raise our teens with a spirit of love, taking care not to aggravate or provoke them, lest they decide to quit trying.

A tall order? You bet. But as we seek God's wisdom for the daily decisions of our lives, parenting in the way he directs and being willing to extend grace to our kids in the same measure that God gives it to us, he will make a way. He is the God of Malachi 4:6, the only One who can turn the hearts of parents to their children, and the hearts of children to their parents.

Turn our hearts, O Lord.

Prayers You Can Use

Heavenly Father . . .

Help me preach your word and be prepared in season and out of season. Show me how to correct, rebuke, and encourage _____—with great patience and careful instruction.

2 Timothy 4:2

Teach me how to set a godly example for _____, and equip them to be like King Solomon, who walked before you in integrity of heart and uprightness, even as his father David did.

1 Kings 9:4

As _____ and I talk with each other, let no unwholesome talk come out of our mouths, but only what is helpful for building each other up according to our needs, that our words may benefit each other and strengthen our relationship. *Ephesians 4:29*

Prompt _____ to listen to correction and not neglect instruction, since what they learn from their parents will crown them with grace and honor. *Proverbs 1:8–9 NLT*

Help me start _____ off in the way they should go, counting on your promise that even when they are old they will not turn from it. *Proverbs 22:6*

Cause _____ to obey all your commands, including the one about honoring parents, and remain in your love so that your joy will be in them and their joy will be complete.

John 15:10–11

As I raise _____, please be my shepherd and lead me, Lord. Gather me in your arms and carry me close to your heart, giving me grace and wisdom as you gently lead "those that have young."

Isaiah 40:11

Make _____ like John the Baptist, a child who brought joy and delight to his parents. Let them bring others back to you, Lord, turning the hearts of fathers to their children and the disobedient to the wisdom of the righteous.   *Luke 1:14–17*

May _____ see discipline as a sign of love and legitimacy in a family. Help them realize that we are doing our best, as parents, and that we ourselves submit to your discipline.

Hebrews 12:6–10

Keep _____'s heart on the right course, not carousing with drunkards or feasting with gluttons but listening to their father, who gave them life. Don't let _____ despise me when I am old—and not so old!   *Proverbs 23:19, 22*

Teach _____ to obey us in everything, for this pleases you. Don't let us do or say anything that would embitter or discourage our teens.   *Colossians 3:20-21*

Turn our heart toward our teens, and turn their hearts toward us.
                                                                    Malachi 4:6

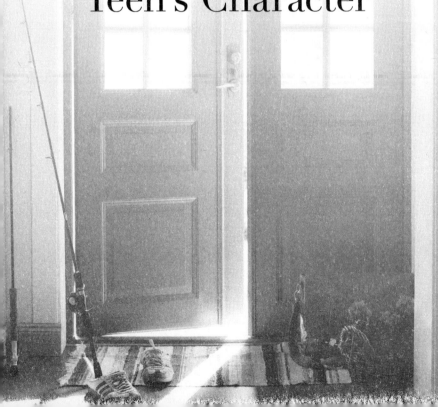

Part 2

Praying for Your Teen's Character

Chapter 6

Praying for Honesty and Integrity

The LORD detests lying lips,
but he delights in those who tell the truth.
Proverbs 12:22 NLT

"Where were you last night?"

Molly eyed her daughter, watching carefully for any hint of deception. Molly's maternal instincts had kicked into overdrive, but she wanted to give Jenna a chance to tell the truth before she confronted her with what she already knew: that Jenna had left a birthday party and then shown up—much later—at a girlfriend's house where she had been invited to spend the night.

"I was at Allie's house."

"How did you get there?"

"Brian drove me there after the party."

Molly had never heard Jenna talk about anyone named Brian, but she had heard—from another mom—that Jenna had left the birthday party with a boy.

"Who's Brian?" Molly asked.

"He's a friend of Allie. He offered to take me to her house."

"Did you kiss him?"

"Mom! What's with all the questions?"

Molly hadn't planned to ask about the kissing; the question had simply popped into her head. And now that Jenna had side-stepped the issue, she sensed she had hit a mark.

"Did you kiss Brian?" she repeated.

"No, Mom!" Jenna scoffed. "*Nothing* happened!"

There it was—the slightest cloud flickered across Jenna's face, signaling to Molly that her daughter was not telling the truth. Molly didn't really care whether or not Jenna had kissed anyone; that wasn't really the issue. It was the lying that mattered—and lately, it seemed that Jenna had been lying about a lot of things. She lied about what she ate; she lied about whose clothing she wore. She even lied about things that didn't make any sense—like when she told a friend she had broken a picture frame when Molly knew she hadn't! Was it a cry for attention? Molly didn't know.

Later that night, Molly turned to her prayer journal. She flipped through the pages, scanning the prayers she had written during the past few months:

Write your word on Jenna's heart, that she may choose to hate sin and love your holiness. The words are based on Psalm 119:9–11. *Gather the wheat in Jenna's life, and burn up the chaff.* Luke 3:17. *Before a word is on her tongue, you know it completely, Lord. Shine your light on the darkness in her life, and lead her in the way everlasting.* A few verses from Psalm 139.

As Molly reread the prayers, she realized she was exhausted. "Father," she prayed, "I am too tired to fight this battle. If Jenna is not telling the truth about kissing Brian, I am going to let it go—but I am trusting you to work in her life and to smash the spirit of lying that is trying to take up residence in her heart."

The prophet Jeremiah would have understood Molly's fatigue, as well as her heartache. Way back when Jeremiah was a teen, about six hundred years before Jesus was born, deception was a way of life among God's people. "Beware of your neighbor!" the prophet warned. "Don't even trust your brother! For brother takes advantage of brother, and friend slanders friend. They all fool and defraud each other; no one tells the truth. With practiced tongues they tell lies; they wear themselves out with all their sinning. They pile lie upon lie and utterly refuse to acknowledge me, says the LORD."[1]

With practiced tongues they tell lies.

There's no question that lying gets easier with practice. And in a world where shifting blame, denying guilt, and withholding key information has become commonplace, it's no surprise that our teens can twist the truth, break promises, and even tell bald-faced lies without feeling like they've hurt anyone or done something wrong. Really, though, the willingness to lie is not a new problem; consider the fact that Cain, history's very first teen, lied to God—*to God!*—after he murdered his brother. "Where is your brother?" God wanted to know. "How should I know?" Cain replied. "Am I supposed to keep track of him wherever he goes?"[2]

PRAYER PRINCIPLE

Lying gets easier with practice. Pray that
your teens will be caught so they don't get
comfortable and familiar with deceit.

When teens lie, it's often for the same reasons adults do: to impress people, to advance themselves (academically, financially, socially, or in some other way), to protect their friends, and—like Cain—to get out of trouble. While these reasons may make lying *understandable*, they never make it *acceptable*. God doesn't wink at deception. Not only did he put lying on his Top Ten list in the Old Testament, but at the end of the New Testament he lumps liars with cowards, murderers, idolaters, and a host of other evil creatures, saying that their place will be in "the fiery lake of burning sulfur."[3] And just in case we need some cake with that icing, he punctuates the rest of the Bible with such words as *hate*, *detest*, and *abhor* to describe how he feels about dishonesty.[4] And why wouldn't God feel this way? Where, after all, do lies come from? From Satan—the one Jesus called "the father of lies"![5]

Peggy is a mom who places a high priority on honesty. She taught her kids that omitting details from a story was the same thing as lying, and she prayed that if they were ever doing anything wrong, their sin (as Numbers 32:23 puts it) would find them out. She wanted her kids to tell the truth, no matter what—and if getting caught was what it took to make them honest, so be it.

Little did Peggy know what would happen when God answered those prayers . . .

ᗧ ᗧ ᗧ

Crash!

The can of soda smashed through the window, spilling its contents onto the living room floor. Car wheels drowned out the sound of the boys' laughter as they sped away. As members of their high school's championship soccer team, they were all too familiar with late-night pranks, and this latest—a stealth attack on the home of their archrival's leading scorer—seemed, in their adolescent minds, to be a brilliant idea.

When Peggy learned that her son, Charlie, had participated in the vandalism, she took a different view. "It was a definite moment of stupidity," she said. "The boys had planned to put Oreos on this fellow's windshield as a practical joke, and the prank got out of hand."

But that was just the beginning. Called into the school office the next day, the boys learned that they had been caught on videotape as they purchased their arsenal of soda and cookies. "Do you want to tell me about it?" the school official asked.

To a man, the other culprits—all considered "team leaders" by their coach and the other players—denied any wrongdoing. Charlie, though, could not keep silent. As an honor student and a well-known leader in his church youth group, he felt he needed to confess. He had no interest in staging any sort of a cover-up, and he fully believed Jesus' words in John 8:31–32: "If you hold to my teaching, you are really my disciples. Then you will know the truth, and the truth will set you free." Charlie had made a mistake; now all he wanted was to set the record straight and make amends.

"You're crazy!" one of his teammates cried, when he learned what Charlie had done.

"What were you thinking?" asked another. "We need to stick together. If you hadn't confessed, they never would have been able to prove we had anything to do with what happened."

Never before had Charlie so keenly felt the pain of rejection. But as it turned out, his teammates' ire was the least of his worries. The man whose house the boys had damaged was not about to settle matters quietly. Rather than accept payment for his broken window and soiled carpet, he decided to go to court—and in the end, Peggy and her husband wound up shelling out more than $10,000 in legal fees. Not only that, but Charlie's conviction—all but assured by his confession—went on his permanent record, and in addition to requiring Charlie to perform 250 hours of community service and attend six months' worth of youth offender classes, the judge ruled that he had to spend three days in jail!

"I cannot begin to describe the pain I felt as I watched my son walk into that jail," Peggy said. "As the gates shut behind him, locking him in with a bunch of felons, I felt like all my dreams for him were shattered. I knew his future would never be the same."

And indeed, Charlie's reputation was tarnished. During Charlie's college application interview, one of the interviewers pulled up his name on the internet and discovered that he had been indicted for a misdemeanor. After a lengthy explanation, Charlie was accepted at the university—but two years later, when he tried to lease an apartment near the campus, he was turned down, based on the results of a routine criminal background check.

"I never dreamed that telling the truth could be so costly," Peggy said. "But I have discovered that, very often, our greatest growth comes from our greatest failures. Charlie has taken responsibility for his life, and he is mature beyond his years. He has compassion for others, and the grace he shows is only that of someone who has experienced the grace of God."

"And," she continued, "*I've* learned some lessons too. I have had to learn how to forgive the man whose desire for vengeance did so much damage to my family. I have learned that just because someone makes a bad decision, they are not a bad person—and they need grace and mercy rather than condemnation and judgment. Most of all, I've learned that, despite what I sometimes think, I am not in control of my teen's journey toward God—but God is always at work in his life."

PRAYER PRINCIPLE

Very often our greatest growth comes
from our greatest failures.

Poised for Prayer

Telling the truth can be costly, but holding on to a lie comes with its own set of direr consequences. Scripture is full of train-wreck stories about lives gone awry as the result of a lie: Rebekah deceived her husband and—for all practical purposes—lost her favorite son. Jacob lied to his father and had to run for his life. Ananias and his wife lied to the early church about money—and dropped dead on the spot![6]

Stories like these can make us shudder. But if you've caught your teen in a lie, or even if lying seems to be your teen's preferred communication style, don't panic. Instead, remember that God clues us in to frightening or worrisome situations not to scare us but to prompt us to pray. This revelation has not come as a surprise to God; trust him to provide as you pray.

Next, try to discover what motivated the lie. Was it fear? Insecurity? A desire to "cover" for friends? Ask God to reveal anything you need to know, and be specific when you pray.

Keep talking about the importance of truthfulness and integrity, modeling these qualities for your kids and looking at the issue from God's perspective. (My friend Lisa is confident that her kids are headed for heaven, but she made them memorize an abbreviated and paraphrased version of Revelation 21:8—"Liars go to hell"—just to keep them on their toes.)

And finally, as you pray, remember where lies originate. Satan is the father of lies, and he likes nothing better than to get us to believe his twisted words—including the lie that our kids are "doomed" or "beyond redemption" when they blow it in a big way. One of the things I liked best about Peggy's story was that she refused to listen to Satan:

She could be living in a prison of bitterness, but she chose to forgive the man who hurt her son.

She could have seen the entire experience as a tragic mess, but she chose to find God's redemptive purposes instead.

She could have beaten herself up over her failure to successfully manage her son's life, but she learned to let God be in control. As my friend Jeannie Cunnion puts it when she talks about her book *Mom Set Free*, "We are significant in our kids' lives, but we are not sovereign."

What about you? What are the lies that Satan is trying to get you to believe?

Has he whispered that your teen is a mess, and that nothing will *ever* change? Has he told you that you've blown it as a parent and that you will *never* get it right? Don't listen! Our ability to ruin our kids is nothing compared to God's power to redeem them. He is not surprised by anything they do, and having started a good work in their lives, he promises to carry it on to completion until the day of Christ Jesus.[7]

If you were to talk to Molly, the mom I mentioned at the beginning of this chapter, she'd tell you that God is definitely at work in Jenna's life. Not only did Jenna confess to—and ask forgiveness for—lying about the kiss (Molly's instincts were right!), but in the past year, the shadows of deception have all but disappeared. Today, she and Jenna enjoy a relationship marked by open communication and truthfulness. "I'm continuing to pray," Molly said, "and I know God continues to work."

Satan may be the father of lies, but Jesus Christ is the Truth. Let's call out to him, trusting in his incomparably great power to change our hearts and set our families free.

Prayers You Can Use

Heavenly Father . . .

A good person produces good things from the treasury of a good heart, and an evil person produces evil things from the treasury of an evil heart. Work in _____'s heart so that good things will flow out.   *Luke 6:45 NLT*

Cause _____ to put off falsehood and speak truthfully, for we are all members of one body.   *Ephesians 4:25*

Keep _____ from deceitful ways. Teach them to choose the way of faithfulness and equip them to hold fast to your statutes so that they will never be put to shame.   *Psalm 119:29–31*

Let _____'s words be truthful so they will stand the test of time. Give them a heart filled with peace and joy instead of deceit.
Proverbs 12:19–20

Keep _____'s tongue from evil and their lips from speaking lies so that they will love life and enjoy good days.
Psalm 34:12–13

You test the heart and are pleased with integrity. May _____'s heart please you, and may all that they say, do, and give be with honest intent. Keep _____'s heart loyal to you.
1 Chronicles 29:17–18

Set a guard over _____'s mouth; keep watch over their lips.

Psalm 141:3

Guard _____'s life and rescue them; let them never be put to shame. May integrity and uprightness protect them and cause them to hope in you.

Psalm 25:20-21

Help _____ to stand firm with the belt of truth buckled securely around their waist and the breastplate of righteousness guarding their heart.

Ephesians 6:14

Cause _____ to be careful to lead a blameless life and have nothing to do with evil. Do not let them slander friends or classmates in secret. Keep _____ from practicing deceit or speaking falsely so that they dwell in your house and stand in your presence.

Psalm 101:2-7

Satan is a liar and the father of lies. Don't allow _____ to listen to Satan or carry out his desires; rather, tune their ears to hear what you say. Let _____ receive and believe the truth you speak, knowing that they belong to you.

John 8:42-47

Let _____ be a truthful witness, knowing that deceit is in the heart of those who plot evil but those who promote peace have joy.

Proverbs 12:17-20

May the words of _____'s mouth and the meditations of their heart be pleasing in your sight.

Psalm 19:14

Cause _____ to hold to your teaching, to be your disciple, and to know the truth that sets us free.

John 8:31–32

Chapter 7

Praying for an Others-Centered Outlook

Do nothing out of selfish ambition or vain
conceit. Rather, in humility value others above
yourselves, not looking to your own interests,
but each of you to the interests of the others.
Philippians 2:3–4

"The world does not revolve around you."

How many times have you said—or at least thought—these words as you looked at your teen? In an informal survey of some of my friends regarding teens and self-centeredness, here's a snippet of what I heard: "My daughter definitely thinks she's 'all that.'" "Right now, my son is the center of his universe." "I just wish she would wake up and realize that there are other people living in our house."

Self-centeredness is, of course, a human condition—teens aren't the only ones who suffer from it. But as Joe White and Jim Weidmann point out in their book *Parents' Guide to the Spiritual Mentoring of Teens*, the teen years tend to bring out an "acuteness of self" and that, if self-centeredness were a disease, "most teens would be diagnosed with at least a mild case, and many would be classified as suffering from 'chronic, inflamed egotism.'"[1]

White is the director of Kanakuk Kamps, a summer camp program designed to give children and teens the opportunity to grow in faith, confidence, and Christian character. The Kanakuk experience is built on putting God first, others second, and yourself third. This "I'm Third" principle comes from Matthew 22:36–40, where Jesus says that the greatest commandment is to love God "with all your heart and with all your soul and with all your mind," and that the second greatest commandment is to "love your neighbor as yourself." Our kids all attended Kanakuk, and every time I see the "I'm Third" sign on Hillary's bedroom mirror, I thank God for the staff and counselors who so beautifully model this way of life for some seventeen thousand campers every summer.[2]

PRAYER PRINCIPLE

Serving others frees our teens from
the burden of self-absorption.

If we want to free our teens from Joe White's diagnosis of "chronic, inflamed egotism" and help them kindle a heart for service, sometimes one of the best things we can do is to get them out of their comfort zones. Our church routinely sends groups of young people on short-term missions to poorer areas of the United States, as well as to such far-flung locations as Tanzania, the Dominican Republic, and China. For some parents, like my friend Michelle, sending a teen to the other side of the world demands mountains of prayer, lots of deep breaths, and an entire suitcase full of things like Band-Aids and hand sanitizer. But even with all of her maternal worries and concerns, Michelle would be the first to tell you that, for her daughter Julia, going to China was an answer to prayer ...

ๆ ๆ ๆ

"Open yours next, Julia!"

Six-year-old Amanda idolized her older sister, and as the family gathered to celebrate the New Year on January 1, she was eager to see what was on Julia's scrap of paper. Twelve months earlier, each family member had written a list of goals for the coming year. Now, clustered around the dining room table, they were ready to revisit these objectives to see what the year—and God—had brought.

Michelle gazed at her fourteen-year-old daughter with a bittersweet mixture of concern, pride, and joy. Her mind wandered back to the previous year, when Julia was in the eighth grade. It had been a tough season. As a student at a small private school, Julia did not have a large peer group, and she had wrestled with loneliness. Keenly aware of her daughter's pain, Michelle had struggled at times to trust God. Now, though, she realized the time Julia had spent alone, hard as it was, had served to deepen her relationship with God and heighten her sensitivity to the emotional needs of others.

It had started, Michelle thought, in China. Julia had gone on a three-week summer mission trip, where she helped run an English language camp for children. In addition to asking God to protect Julia and the other team members, Michelle prayed that her daughter would be a blessing to others, that she would find a special friend in China, and—knowing that the language barrier could pose a problem—that the spiritual language of God's love would flow out of the American teens and into the hearts of the Chinese children.

Unable to communicate with her daughter for three long weeks left Michelle hungry for information, and when the group returned, she couldn't wait to hear all the details. And Julia couldn't wait to share them. She stayed up almost all night long, tears streaming down her face, recounting story after story of the Chinese people and her love for them. One girl, in particular, had captured Julia's heart. Despite her own obvious material needs, little "Abby" had insisted on giving Julia her favorite bracelet as a token of their friendship. "The Chinese children had so little," Julia observed, "but they gave so much. It was amazing."

Abby—who, like the other Chinese children, had chosen an English name that the mission team could remember and pronounce—represented the answer to Michelle's prayer for Julia to find a friend. But there was more. Suddenly, Julia's desire for friends and activity-filled weekends didn't matter as much as it had before. Working with Abby and the other Chinese children had opened Julia's eyes to the joy that comes through serving others. Never had she felt so close to Jesus.

PRAYER PRINCIPLE

Asking God to give your teens a heart for service
is asking him to connect them to Christ.

Julia resolved to find a place where she could minister in a similar way closer to home. When she learned that her church was sponsoring a back-to-school party for a group of underprivileged children, Julia jumped in, raising more than $800 to help fill backpacks with school supplies. When she realized that the kids and their families had very little warm clothing for the winter, she organized a "Blanket the Neighborhood" drive to supply them with blankets, clothing, and shoes. And later, when she learned of a mentoring program that existed to serve those same families, Julia quickly got on board. She and Lainey, her "little sister," became fast friends—so much so that Julia had invited Lainey to join their family's New Year's Day celebration.

"Yeah, Julia, open your paper!" Lainey urged, joining Amanda's cries and drawing Michelle's attention back to the party. "We want to see what you wrote."

Slowly, Julia unfolded the paper. It seemed hard to believe that a whole year had passed since she had last seen her goals. "I want to become more self-confident," she read aloud.

That one, Michelle noted, had definitely happened. Whether Julia realized it or not, her decision to focus on others instead of herself had given her a newfound sense of purpose and peace.

"I want to do a good cause."

"Well, you blanketed the neighborhood," Amanda pointed out. "You can check that one off."

Julia's next resolution drew a round of laughter: "I want to walk the dog." And then came one that pierced Michelle's heart: "I want to get more friends."

Here again, God had come through. Julia had started her ninth-grade year at a new school—one that brought with it a group of new friends and an increasingly full social calendar.

"Are there any more things on your list?" Lainey asked.

"Just one," Julia answered. "I said that I want to change someone's life."

For a moment, nobody spoke. And then Lainey looked over at the piece of paper and read Julia's words for herself. She looked up, her big brown eyes speaking words she could not express.

"You've changed *my* life," she said softly.

Just as God, Michelle realized, had changed Julia's.

Poised for Prayer

I love Michelle's family tradition of writing down goals or prayer requests every year and then ushering in the New Year with thanksgiving. But New Year's Day isn't the only time she reflects on God's goodness. Michelle logs her own prayers in a journal, and when I interviewed her for this chapter, she was able to look back and see God's track record—tangible evidence that he had heard the deepest cries of her heart.

Michelle's kids are all girls, yet they are very different people. *Does Michelle*, I wondered, *have any favorite prayers that worked for each of them?*

"I love to pray for the Holy Spirit's presence," she said. "When I open my prayer journal in the morning, I ask God to show me if there is any aspect of the Holy Spirit's fruit that one or another of my girls might need in extra measure that day. One day they might need extra kindness or love. Another day might call for peace and joy. Or God might prompt me to pray for things like patience, gentleness, or self-control.[3]

"I can't know what my children will need at any given moment," she said. "But God does—and when I invite the Holy Spirit to work in their lives, I know they will be prepared for whatever comes their way."

Whether you are praying for an end to the "me, myself, and I" attitude, or whether your prayers are for something else entirely, I want to encourage you to follow Michelle's example. If you're not already doing so, start keeping a prayer journal. You can pour out your heart over three or four pages, or just grab a Scripture or two from any of the chapters in this book and jot them down, bullet-point style. Try this for a month, and you'll see the fingerprints of God's provision. Try it for a year, and things you forgot you even cared or prayed about will be there, in black-and-white, for you to see. And then, as you reflect on God's goodness, you'll be equipped to follow Paul's charge: "Tell God your needs, and don't forget to thank him for his answers."[4]

And as you pray, let your teen know what you're doing. I'll never forget the time our daughter Virginia "caught" me sitting up in bed with a copy of *Praying the Scriptures for Your Children* open on my lap. She bounded into the room, took one look, and laughed out loud. "You're reading your own book?" she teased. "Mom, that's just so *sad*!"

Virginia laughed when she was a teen; now, she asks me to pray—for her and for her friends.

Hang in there, Mom and Dad. Even if your teen doesn't put much stock in prayer now, the image—the memory—of seeing their earthly parent talk to their heavenly Parent is something that will inform their own prayer life down the road. It will equip them to live out Philippians 2:4, looking beyond their own interests as they bring the needs of their friends, family, and coworkers to the Lord.

Prayers You Can Use

Heavenly Father . . .

Fill _____ with your Holy Spirit. Let their words and deeds be marked by love, joy, peace, patience, kindness, goodness, faithfulness, gentleness, and self-control.

Galatians 5:22–23 NLT

Let _____ put you first, others second, and themselves third. May they love you with all of their heart, soul, and mind and love others as themselves.

Matthew 22:37–39

Turn _____'s heart toward your statutes and not toward selfish gain.

Psalm 119:36

May no act of service or kindness seem too small in _____'s eyes. May they not despise small beginnings but remember that you rejoice to see good work begin.

Zechariah 4:10 NLT

Cause _____ to follow the example of Jesus, who came not to be served, but to serve.

Matthew 20:28

Let _____ do nothing out of selfish ambition or vain conceit but, in humility, to value others—family, friends, classmates—above themselves. May _____ not look to their own interests but look beyond to focus on the needs of other people.

Philippians 2:3–4

Teach _____ to honor you by being kind to the needy.

Proverbs 14:31

Make _____ wise and understanding. Let the evidence of these traits be seen in good deeds done in humility.

James 3:13

Cause _____'s life to be marked by love—the kind that is patient and kind and never envious, boastful, proud, rude, or self-seeking.

1 Corinthians 13: 4–5

Remind _____ that when they reach out with food, clothing, hospitality, and other evidences of your love, whatever they do for "the least of these brothers and sisters" is for you.

Matthew 25:34–40

Impress on _____'s heart the need to pair words and beliefs with actions—the kind of good deeds and selfless actions that prove faith is real.

James 2:14–17

Equip _____ to defend the cause of the weak and fatherless and to protect the rights of the poor and the oppressed.

Psalm 82:3

Open _____'s ears to the cries of a world in need and show them how to help.

Proverbs 21:13

May _____ seek to bring glory to you rather than to themself. Let them never seek their own good but the good of many, as Jesus did.   *1 Corinthians 10:31–11:1*

Make _____ enriched in every way so that they can be generous on every occasion, which will result in people giving thanks to you.   *2 Corinthians 9:11*

Chapter 8

Praying for a Humble, Teachable Heart

Remind the people to be subject to rulers and authorities,
to be obedient, to be ready to do whatever is good,
to slander no one, to be peaceable and considerate,
and always to be gentle toward everyone.

Titus 3:1–2

"Life's not fair."

If this isn't one of the most trotted-out lines in the history of parenting, I don't know what is. I've used it on my kids when refs make questionable calls, when teachers impose extra-tough grading standards, and when my husband and I say no to something our teens don't agree with or understand.

I'll never forget the day our son, Robbie, came home from basketball practice with his nose out of joint. His coach had awarded a prize to one of the players for making the most free throws—and Robbie was convinced he had seen the fellow step over the line. "It's not fair," Robbie said. "He cheated!"

"Life's not fair," I countered. "Especially in sports. There are going to be ball hogs on your team, bad calls from refs, and coaching decisions you don't understand or agree with. How you respond to these things says a lot about who you are as a player—and as a person."

"Well, it's not right," Robbie muttered, before heading off to do his homework.

Later that night, the subject came up again. "Mom," Robbie said, "I keep going over that shot in my mind. I asked God to help me realize that Austin didn't cheat—but every time I remember the shot, I think he did!"

"Maybe he did," I sighed. "But maybe that's not the point. Maybe God is giving you this opportunity to give up your right to be right. Maybe he wants you to learn to honor your coach and humbly accept his decision—even though that's not the way *you* would have done it."

I was on a roll. "You know," I continued, "the Bible says that God's ways are not our ways.[1] What if we questioned God every time he did something we didn't understand or agree with?"

"But God is God. Of *course* he does stuff we don't understand!"

"I know!" I said with a laugh. "But I think he uses people like coaches—or parents or teachers or bosses—to help us practice accepting the things we may not understand. He wants us to be humble and teachable instead of being stubborn or proud or wanting to quit or argue when things don't go the way we think they should. If you can learn to honor your coaches and your teachers—even if you don't always agree with them—then you will be able to respect God and obey him, even when you don't understand or agree with one of his commands."

I thought it was one of my better parenting speeches. I could see the wheels turning in Robbie's mind, and I hoped he could follow my logic—but I worried that what he was really doing was replaying Austin's shot for the umpteenth time in his head. "Do you see what I mean?" I finally asked.

"I guess so," Robbie said slowly.

And that, I realized, was as good as it was going to get.

A few months later, I remembered my conversation with Robbie when I got a phone call from a girlfriend who had just returned from a round of college recruiting visits with her soccer phenom of a daughter.

"One coach told me they aren't just looking at the players' stats—how many assists they have, how many goals they score, or how many state championships they've won," my friend said. "When they send scouts to a game, they don't just watch the players *on* the field; they watch to see how a girl reacts when she is pulled *off* the field. Does she sulk? Sit at the end of the bench? Roll her eyes? Ignore the coaches? Get on her cell phone? Does she—"

"Do players *really* get on their cell phones during a game?" I interrupted.

"Oh, you'd be surprised. But that's not the point. The point is that the college scouts are looking for players who are open to correction and who are willing to make changes.

"And you know what?" my friend continued. "I think that's how God looks at us. He watches us to see how we respond to correction and how we react when things don't go our way."

Wow. Maybe Robbie hadn't totally connected the dots between his relationship to his coach and his relationship to God, but my girlfriend had, and that was all the inspiration I needed to redouble my prayer efforts for my kids to have humble, teachable hearts—whether they're on the athletic field, in the classroom, or just sitting around our dinner table.

PRAYER PRINCIPLE

Asking God to give our teens a teachable heart in school equips them to receive his correction in life.

God loves it when we ask him to give our kids a humble, teachable heart. A couple of years after *Praying the Scriptures for Your Children* was released, a mom at church pulled me aside and told me what God had done in her son's life . . .

༚ ༚ ༚

"I'm having some problems with Ryan."

Melanie knew the teacher on the other end of the telephone was serious, but she was the PE teacher, for goodness' sake. How bad could the problems be?

"He's trying to run the class," the woman explained.

"Oh." Melanie didn't know what to say. "I'll talk to him about it," she offered.

"Thanks," the teacher said. "Ryan is a very talented young man—and he's extremely competitive. I love the fact that he always gives it everything he has, but the trouble is that he doesn't take correction very well."

Melanie knew exactly what the teacher meant. Ryan was a strong athlete, and he had been able to get away with some sloppy habits. But as other players honed their skills, they were sure to catch up with him—and if the lack of finesse didn't sideline him one day, Melanie worried that Ryan's stubborn attitude would.

She picked up her copy of *Praying the Scriptures for Your*

Children and flipped to the back of the chapter that targeted kids' relationships with teachers and coaches.

> Cause _____ to have confidence in teachers and coaches and submit to their authority, since they will be accountable to you for the job they do. May _____ make their work a joy, not a burden.

That prayer, rooted in Hebrews 13:17, reflected the desire of Melanie's heart. She mentally inserted Ryan's name into the blanks and then called her son into the room, showing him what she had prayed.

"God wants you to listen to your PE teacher," she said. "God says that when you make her job a joy instead of a burden, it will wind up being a good thing for you in the end."

Ryan knew his mother meant business. She was giving him an opportunity to respond to his teacher's correction. He could take it or leave it. He decided to take it.

It wasn't long before Melanie happened to see the PE teacher at school. "Hey!" the teacher said. "You won't believe what's happened. Ryan's attitude has totally turned around—it's like a miracle!"

Melanie was thrilled, but she found herself back on her knees a couple of years later when Ryan's younger brothers found themselves in the same teacher's class. Like their older brother, the boys made no secret of their impatience with the woman's coaching methods. Couldn't she see that they knew how the games ought to be played?

Melanie knew that the God who had worked such a change in Ryan's life could do the same for her other boys. "Lord," she prayed, "cause Wilson and Spencer to obey their teacher and submit to her authority." She finished praying Hebrews 13:17 again and continued to ask God to work in her younger sons' lives as they grew.

Melanie had a sense that God was answering her prayers (she wasn't getting any phone calls from frustrated teachers), but nothing could have prepared her for the surprise that lay in store. At the graduation ceremony, two students were honored for the "Most Improved Sportsmanship" award—Wilson and Spencer! Thinking of the last few words in Hebrews 13:17—that when our kids obey their leaders and submit to their authority, the end result will be to their benefit—Melanie couldn't help but marvel at the goodness of God.

PRAYER PRINCIPLE

When we pray for our teens to humbly
submit to authority, we are setting
them up to reap God's rewards.

Poised for Prayer

The Bible is brimming with examples of folks who were willing to submit to God and learn from him. Moses, for instance, was known as "a very humble man, more humble than anyone else on the face of the earth."[2] There are also plenty of examples of people exalting themselves and refusing to acknowledge God's authority—folks like King Nebuchadnezzar, who spent seven years eating grass like a wild animal because of his own arrogance and pride.[3]

On the humble roster, I find myself drawn to John the Baptist. As a young locust-eater, John was no stranger to recognition—crowds jostled to get near him, and he had a posse of disciples who were bigger fans than any clique of high school cheerleaders. But when the curiosity seekers and autograph hounds demanded to know who he was and tried to get him to talk about himself, he did not take the bait. Instead, he continually talked about Jesus, saying that he was someone whose sandals he, John, was not worthy even to untie.

Ultimately, when Jesus showed up, John was the first to recognize him. Had I been John, I think I would have told all of my friends that "I saw him first!" My story would have gotten better with each telling, until my accomplishment—spotting the Lord—threatened to eclipse Jesus' very appearance. But not John. John admitted that he recognized Jesus when he saw the Holy Spirit descend on him in the form of a dove—but he quickly pointed out that he would never have known what it all meant had God not clued him in as to what to look for.[4]

I love John's humility. Had he been an athlete, I bet he would have had the all-time record for assists, only we'd never know it because he would get us to spend so much time looking at Jesus—the leading scorer—that we'd forget all about his accomplishments. Had he been a musician, I bet he would have been willing to play second fiddle, providing the harmony to complement—and never overpower—the guy who sat in the first chair. Had he been an actor, I bet he would have made sure to turn the spotlight, and the loudest applause, on the one who directed the play.

"Before a downfall the heart is haughty," says Proverbs 18:12, "but humility comes before honor." When I pray for my teens, I pray that they will be like John the Baptist—a man who had plenty to be proud of, but who chose humility instead. I pray that they will never seek glory or attention for themselves, but that they will give credit to others. Most of all, I pray that they will show respect for their teachers, coaches, and peers—whether they are serving on the student council or sitting in the back row of a math class—so their character and their conduct will bring honor to Jesus.

Prayers like these can feel like big asks. To resist authority and seek honor and attention for yourself is human nature—and believe me, our family is *plenty* human. But as I pray for my teens—and as you pray for yours—we can do so knowing that we serve a God who delights in those who honor him and who is able to do immeasurably more in our kids' lives than all we ask or imagine.[5]

Prayers You Can Use

Heavenly Father . . .

May _____ be submissive to authority, obedient, and ready for every good work. May they speak evil of no one, avoid quarreling, be gentle, and show perfect courtesy toward all people.

Titus 3:1–2 ESV

Let _____ give you praise and glory for their talents and abilities, knowing that everything they have comes from you.

1 Chronicles 29:11–14

May _____ delight in your word, since it is useful for teaching, rebuking, correcting, and training in righteousness. Equip _____ for every good work.   *2 Timothy 3:16–17*

Cause _____ to be submissive and respectful toward those who are older and more experienced. Let them be clothed with humility, remembering that you oppose the proud but give grace to the humble, and that you will lift them up in due time.

1 Peter 5:5–6

May _____ act justly, love mercy, and walk humbly with you, since this is what you require.   *Micah 6:8*

Help _____ to do nothing out of selfish ambition or vain conceit. Cause them to treat coaches and teammates with humility, thinking not of their own interests, but giving others support and credit. *Philippians 2:3–4*

Let _____ be honest in their estimate of themselves, measuring value not by worldly success but by the faith you give. Open their eyes to see and appreciate the different gifts and talents you have given to others. *Romans 12:3–6*

Remind _____ that pride goes before destruction, and a haughty spirit before a fall. *Proverbs 16:18*

Give _____ confidence in their leaders and help them submit to authority so that the leaders' work will be a joy, not a burden, for that would be of no benefit to them. *Hebrews 13:17*

Cause _____ to be wise in the way they act toward coaches, teachers, and other authorities. Let them make the most of every opportunity, using words that are gracious and effective, so that nothing will bring dishonor to your name. *Colossians 4:5–6*

Prompt _____ to acknowledge that you rule over the kingdoms of the world and appoint anyone you desire to rule over them. *Daniel 5:21 NLT*

Teach _____ to listen to advice and accept instruction so that they will be wise. *Proverbs 19:20*

Don't let _____ lose heart when you rebuke them; remind them that you discipline those you love.   *Hebrews 12:5-6*

May _____ take your yoke and learn from you, for you are gentle and humble in heart.   *Matthew 11:29*

Chapter 9

Praying through Anger
to Composure

Better to be patient than powerful;
*   better to have self-control than to conquer a city.*
Proverbs 16:32 NLT

"Is it a sin to get angry?"

I posed the question to our four children as we sat around the dinner table one night. I wasn't sure how they'd respond and—in an effort to keep them from influencing one another's opinions—I called for a quick "up or down" vote, no talking allowed.

Is it a sin to get angry?

Two kids said yes; two said no.

My question stemmed from a conversation I'd had with a high school counselor who had worked with countless teens and their families—people representing a wide range of spiritual beliefs and convictions. As we discussed anger, he told me that in some of the Christian families he has counseled, kids are so afraid to express their anger—fearing it is a sin and something that has no place in a Christian's life—that they bottle it up until they can't hold it in any longer and it comes out in destructive ways: things like bad attitudes, unkind or negative remarks, and violence.

I cringed when I heard that, wondering about my own kids, and when 50 percent of them flunked my pop quiz, I hurried to do some damage control. "Anger is not a sin," I told them. "The Bible says we aren't supposed to be easily offended or quick-tempered, and that when someone—or something—makes us mad, we can't let the situation go unresolved. But all of us have times when we get mad; that's just part of life."

As is often the case when I think I'm teaching the kids an important lesson, they didn't seem to be all that impressed by my insights. "Okay," one of them said, "anger isn't a sin. Can I have the last roll?"

Anger can be a tricky subject. We *ought* to get angry at the things that mar God's glory—things like child abuse, adultery, and ethnic or social injustice—but when our anger stems from our own sinfulness, selfishness, or pride, it has no place in our lives. When it comes to helping our teens deal with their anger, the problem can be complicated by the fact that we may not know what's making them mad. Sometimes they don't either! It could be an argument with a friend or a rejection (real or imagined) by one of their peers. It could be a hurt that hasn't healed—maybe from a divorce that happened five years ago or from harsh words spoken yesterday. It could be the result of unmet expectations or of some sort of anxiety, such as worrying that they'll fail a test or get cut from a team.

PRAYER PRINCIPLE

When our teen is angry, we may not understand why. But that's okay, because God does.

Sometimes we will be able to discover what lies behind our teen's anger; sometimes we won't. The good news is that God knows. He "searches every heart and understands every desire and every thought."[1] He knows what makes our kids tick—and what ticks them off—and when we bring our concerns before his throne, he will show us exactly how we should pray . . .

ॐ ॐ ॐ

Sandy hung up the phone and turned to her husband, Jay, torn between anger and shame. Had their son really been arrested?

"How could he do such a thing?" Sandy cried out.

Andrew, who was away at college, had evidently gotten into an argument with his girlfriend. The exchange had grown heated, and in a fit of rage he had pushed her, causing her to fall. Onlookers had called the police.

"I just can't believe it," Sandy said. "I mean, he's never done *anything* like this before."

Jay understood Sandy's frustration, but like her, he had no answers. Years ago, when Andrew was still in middle school, they had taken him to a counselor, who had assured them that their son's occasional negativity and tendency toward sarcasm were fairly normal traits in adolescent boys. They had been reassured, but they continued to pray for Andrew's character development as he grew.

College had ushered in a new host of concerns, not the least of which was the alcohol that seemed to pervade almost every aspect of campus life. Andrew didn't always make the best choices, but he had never been violent. Theirs was a family marked by mutual respect, and Andrew and his younger siblings had all the love they could ever want—not to mention every other physical and spiritual advantage. Sandy was certain that, in their home at least, Andrew had never, ever been exposed to any sort of physical abuse. Why, she and Jay hardly ever even raised their voices!

In the days that followed Andrew's arrest, Sandy's emotions ran the gamut from anger (she was horrified by her son's actions) to shame (how could he have come from their family?) to despair. Sandy pored over the pages in her Bible, desperate to know how God could ever use such an ugly, painful incident for good.

One of her favorite prayers came from 2 Corinthians 10:4–5, a passage she had been praying over Andrew for about seven years. "Lord," she prayed again, "demolish the strongholds in Andrew's life. Demolish arguments and every pretension that sets itself up against the knowledge of you. Take all of Andrew's thoughts and make them obedient to Christ."

Sandy thought about the strongholds she had prayed against over the years—those mental, emotional, and spiritual fortresses that had seemed, from time to time, to capture Andrew's mind. She had prayed about pride, rebellion, depression, fear, and even materialism. She had asked God to protect her son and to keep his heart and mind free from Satan's lies. God had answered those prayers, she knew, but something was missing.

Two days later, Sandy was driving to church, crying out to God and asking him—for what seemed like the millionth time—to please do *something* in Andrew's life. Suddenly, almost as clearly as if he were sitting in the seat next to her, she heard God's voice. "Sandy," the Lord said, "all these years you have been praying for the strongholds to come down in Andrew's life. Now, you know how to name the stronghold. It is anger. Pray—and *watch me pull it down.*"

PRAYER PRINCIPLE

When you ask God to demolish something
ugly in your teen's life, name the stronghold
and trust him to pull it down.

There it was—the ray of hope that Sandy needed. She began to pray with a renewed fervor, specifically asking God to tear down the fortress of anger that held Andrew captive. And slowly but surely he did.

It has been more than a year since Sandy began praying specifically about Andrew's anger. During that time, she and Jay have watched their son confront his past mistakes, both via a court-ordered anger management program and through a good dose of self-introspection. He has experienced genuine remorse, repenting of both attitudes and actions. The early transformation has been so remarkable that Sandy and Jay asked Andrew to undergo some psychological testing, just to be certain that no other problems were hidden under their son's newfound peace and humility.

"Andrew is still a work in progress," Sandy told me, "but I'm blown away by all that God has done in his heart and in his life. Jay and I still don't really understand the source of Andrew's anger. It is mysterious to us—but not to God. And I believe that as Andrew continues to grow in the Lord, our understanding—and his healing—will continue. We are amazed at the difference we see in our son every day.

"And more importantly," she concluded, "so is he."

Poised for Prayer

Anger, as my kids will now tell you, is not a sin. Nor is it something that will prevent our teen from being used by God—just look at the apostle Peter! When Jesus met Peter, his very first words were, "Come, follow me." He repeated that command during their last recorded conversation, saying, "You must follow me!"[2] In between these bookends—and for the rest of Peter's earthly life—he did exactly that. He was a guy who cursed and swore, who thought he could rebuke the Lord, and who whipped out his sword and sliced off a soldier's ear when the Pharisees came to arrest Jesus.[3] He was hardly a model citizen—and yet, with all of his failings, Peter managed to stumble and leap and sink and grab his way toward Jesus. He didn't dwell on his outbursts or his flaws; he simply followed Jesus.

We can teach our teens to do the same thing. Scripture outlines a beautiful and effective prescription for dealing with anger. Consider how Ephesians 4:26–27 reads in the following three translations:

- New International Version: "'In your anger do not sin': Do not let the sun go down while you are still angry, and do not give the devil a foothold."
- New Living Translation: "And 'don't sin by letting anger control you.' Don't let the sun go down while you are still angry, for anger gives a foothold to the devil."
- New American Standard Bible: "'Be angry, and yet do not sin'; do not let the sun go down on your anger, and do not give the devil an opportunity."

I like those plainspoken words: *Be angry, and yet do not sin*. Anger, in other words, is not the problem. The problem is sin—the sin that can happen when our kids allow anger to have free rein over their thoughts and actions. "I explode, and then it's all over with" is not an okay explanation. Like the blast of a shotgun, anger can leave a big hole behind. And left unattended, anger can burn out of control, consuming friendships and destroying both tangible and intangible things of value. Even more frightening, it gives Satan the chance he wants—the chance he *craves*—to rip jagged and painful holes in our kids' lives.

Throughout the Bible, the pattern is clear: If we are angry with someone, our job is not to get even or to nurse a grudge or even to simply ignore the problem; our job is to try to make things right. As we pray for our teens in this critical area, let's point them toward the solution outlined in Romans 12:17–21. Let's pray:

- that they would behave honorably, never repaying anyone evil for evil, but being careful to do the right thing;
- that they would do everything in their power to live at peace with others, knowing that when they do their part, the results are up to God;
- that they would never try to take revenge, but that they would let God—whose wrath always includes his mercy—be the one to repay those who deserve it;
- that they would channel their anger into blessings, looking for ways to provide good things for those who have wronged them, that their enemies might be ashamed of their past actions;

- that they would never be controlled by anger or let evil get the best of them, but that they would be empowered by the Holy Spirit to overcome evil with good.

The Bible is full of passages such as these, as well as stories and illustrations that underscore the value of things such as praying for our enemies and living at peace with others. It also has plenty of stories about folks who got angry and lost their cool, just like Peter did.

As we pray for our teens, then, let's keep the picture of Peter in mind. He might have been rash and hot-tempered, but he got it right in the end, urging other Christians to be self-controlled, to show respect to others, to bear up under the pain of unjust suffering, and—I love this one—to never "repay evil with evil or insult with insult" but instead to "repay evil with blessing."[4]

That is the life to which our teens are called. And as it is with all of God's commands, it's doable with the Spirit's help, even for the most hot-tempered among us. All it takes is a willingness to do just what Peter did: follow Jesus—and when we stumble or fall, to get up and follow again.[5]

Prayers You Can Use

Heavenly Father . . .

Teach _____ how to be just like you—compassionate and gracious, slow to anger, abounding in love and faithfulness.

Psalm 86:15

Don't let _____ be like a fool who gives full vent to rage, but cause them to be wise and bring calm. *Proverbs 29:11*

When _____ gets angry, do not let them sin or let the sun go down on their anger and thereby give the devil a foothold.

Ephesians 4:26–27

Get rid of all bitterness, rage, anger, brawling, slander and every form of malice in _____'s life. *Ephesians 4:31*

Cause _____ to be quick to listen, slow to speak, and slow to become angry, because anger does not produce the righteousness you desire. *James 1:19–20*

Let _____'s life be marked by love—the kind that is not easily angered and keeps no record of wrongs. *1 Corinthians 13:5*

Show _____ that when they lash out in anger, calling someone a fool, they put themselves in danger. Let _____ be quick to be reconciled with anyone who has anything against them.

Matthew 5:23–24

Do not allow _____ to repay evil with evil or insult with insult, but respond to offenses with blessings so as to inherit the blessing your promise.

1 Peter 3:9

Demolish the stronghold of anger in _____'s life. Equip _____ to take captive every thought and make it obedient to Christ. *2 Corinthians 10:4–5*

Help _____ to get rid of all anger, rage, malice, slander, and filthy language, being clothed instead with compassion, kindness, humility, gentleness, patience, and love. Cause _____ to bear with others and quickly forgive grievances.

Colossians 3:8–13

Equip _____ to live by the Spirit and not live to gratify the desires of the sinful nature. Fill _____ with the Holy Spirit's fruit, including peace, gentleness, and self-control.

Galatians 5:19–22

May _____ not repay evil for evil, but make every effort to live at peace with everyone and look for ways to overcome evil with good. *Romans 12:17–21*

Guard _____'s heart against the desire to take revenge. Let them be content to leave room for your wrath, knowing that it is up to you to avenge and repay.

Romans 12:19

Bless _____ with strength and peace.   *Psalm 29:11*

May grace and peace be _____'s in abundance through the knowledge of God and of Jesus our Lord.

                                                                 2 Peter 1:2

Chapter 10

Praying for Compassion and Kindness

Be kind and compassionate to one another.
Ephesians 4:32

When I began working on this book, I contacted some friends who work at the Moms in Prayer International headquarters in California.[1] I knew they were well acquainted with the idea of using Bible verses to help shape their prayers, and I figured that, stationed as they are in the epicenter of an international network of praying moms, they would have plenty of stories to share. Sure enough, within a week, my email in-box was loaded with replies.

If you are a parent who bought this book because you wanted to know how to pray about things like "sex, drugs, and rock 'n' roll," I want to assure you that I'm right there with you. Our teens need those "crisis control" kinds of prayers. But they also need our prayers for everyday challenges—things like humility in victory, perseverance in difficulty, and kindness in the face of opportunity.

Sprinkled among the stories in my in-box was this little gem from a mom named Marlae. Hers is not the kind of answered prayer that would make headlines; rather, it highlights the importance of talking to God about the unremarkable—sometimes unseen—things that can go unnoticed in the blur that is teen life. As you read Marlae's story, I hope you'll find it as encouraging as I did.

PRAYER PRINCIPLE

Don't wait for a crisis to prompt you to pray for your teen; ask God to work in the everyday things.

Marlae picked up the phone and cocked her head, nestling the receiver between her shoulder and her ear as she opened the refrigerator. "Hello," she said, placing a gallon of milk on the shelf.

"Hi, Marlae," came a voice she did not recognize. "You might not remember me, but my daughter Ashley is in Joshua's class at school. You'll probably think I'm crazy for calling, but I just had to tell you what Ashley said about your son."

Marlae's hand paused as she pulled a bunch of carrots out of the grocery bag. She wondered what the caller would say.

"Ashley said that Joshua is one of the kindest guys she knows at school. He takes time to say hello to all of the kids in the hallway—not just the ones who are popular. I just thought you'd want to know."

Marlae wanted to laugh out loud. Not two days earlier she had prayed for her seventeen-year-old son, using words from Ephesians 4:32: "May Joshua be kind and compassionate to others, forgiving others just as you forgave us in Christ." At six foot three, Joshua didn't *look* like a meek or compassionate soul, but that didn't stop Marlae from asking God to fill her son with these attributes.

As she thanked the caller and hung up the phone, Marlae's mind wandered back four years to a time when Joshua was not quite so tall—or so confident. Like most thirteen-year-old boys, Josh was a little unsure of himself, particularly when it came to knowing how to act around girls. Marlae worried that the pressure to be "cool" might keep her son from being a good friend to his classmates. She wanted him to be kind and compassionate to everyone—boys and girls, popular kids and misfits. Knowing the power that came with praying the Scriptures, she prayed for Joshua according to 1 Thessalonians 5:15, that he would never "pay back wrong for wrong, but always strive to do what is good."

A few weeks later, Joshua came home from school with a story that seemed to answer that exact prayer. A group of seventh graders were playing in a field that had not been recently mowed when suddenly they heard a sharp cry. Looking around, Joshua saw a girl sitting on the ground, holding her leg. She'd hurt herself on a stick that had been hiding in the tall grass, and even at a distance, Joshua could tell the wound was serious. Blood covered the girl's hands and ran down to her shoe.

For a moment, nobody moved. Joshua hardly knew the girl, and as he looked at his friends, he could tell they were as uncomfortable as he was. But he knew he couldn't just stand there.

"Are you okay?" he asked, hurrying to where the girl sat.

"No," she whimpered. "I can't walk."

"Well, we need to get you to the nurse's office," Joshua said. "Do you think you can climb onto my back?"

Wiping her tears on her sleeve, the girl nodded her head. As he helped her to her feet, Joshua realized she was much bigger than he was. He staggered under her weight but managed to regain his footing. Walking past his friends, he carried the girl into the school.

Marlae found herself smiling as she turned her attention back to her groceries. She pictured her son as a spindly thirteen-year-old, struggling to show kindness to a classmate—and a *girl*, to boot! God certainly had a good sense of humor—and a beautiful way of answering a mother's prayers.

Poised for Prayer

I love Marlae's story because it shows how our hopes and desires for our kids' lives often remain unchanged, even as they grow up and mature. Marlae prayed that her son would be kind when he was just thirteen, and then—even as Joshua evidenced kindness and compassion in answer to those prayers—she continued to lay that request before God's throne. I wouldn't be surprised to see Marlae praying that very same prayer when Joshua is twenty-five or thirty, asking God to equip her son with a tenderness toward his wife or a genuine concern for his coworkers or his children. As praying parents, we can delight in asking God to keep the floodgates of blessing wide open throughout our children's lives!

I also love Marlae's story because it illustrates an important principle about faith. Very often, it's easier to ask God for something when we have already seen him move in answer to prayer than when we are "flying blind"—living and praying by *faith* and not, as 2 Corinthians 5:7 puts it, by *sight*. When God shows up—as he did in answer to Marlae's prayer when Joshua was thirteen years old—it emboldens us to meet future prayer challenges with confidence. We believe God because we have seen what he can do.

But what about those times when we don't have a "prayer precedent"? What if we haven't seen God work in answer to our prayers—or what if he allows something to happen that is definitely *not* the answer we wanted? Where, then, do we place our faith?

The one place where we can put our trust—the one place where we can know that our faith will never be shaken—is in the character of God. Not in *what* he has done but in *who* he is. The Bible shows us a God who is good. It testifies to a God who is powerful. A God who is trustworthy, dependable, and unchanging. A God who loves us more than life itself—because he *is* love itself.

PRAYER PRINCIPLE

Faith enables us to pray with confidence—even when we can't see God working—because our prayers are based not on what God has done but on who he is.

In Exodus 3:13, right after the Lord shows up in the burning bush, Moses asks God to tell him his name. God says, "I AM WHO I AM. This is what you are to say to the Israelites: 'I AM has sent me to you.'"

If you are looking for a place to put your faith—whether you are praying through a relatively "low drama" season of your teen's life or a full-fledged crisis—put it in the God of Exodus 3:14, the One who is known as "I AM." Put it in the God of Psalm 145:13, the One who is "trustworthy in all he promises and faithful in all he does." Put it in the God of Lamentations 3:22, the One whose mercy never fails. Put it in the God of Philippians 1:6, the One who promises that he will be faithful to complete the good work he has begun in our teens.

Put your faith in the God who identifies himself as "I AM."

Prayers You Can Use

Heavenly Father . . .

May _____ follow your example, being compassionate and gracious, slow to anger, and abounding in love.

Psalm 103:8

Cause _____ to be like you are—kind to the ungrateful and the wicked, doing good to them without expecting to get anything back.

Luke 6:35

Comfort _____ in all their troubles, so that they can comfort others in their time of need.

2 Corinthians 1:4

Let _____ open their arms to the poor and extend their hands to the needy.

Proverbs 31:20

Remind _____ that whoever oppresses the poor shows contempt for their Maker, but whoever is kind to the needy honors God.

Proverbs 14:31

May _____ never pay back wrong for wrong but strive to do what is good for everyone else.

1 Thessalonians 5:15

Clothe _____ with compassion, kindness, humility, gentleness, and patience.

Colossians 3:12

Let _____ be kind and compassionate to others, forgiving them, just as in Christ God forgave them.

Ephesians 4:32

Fill _____ with your Holy Spirit's kindness, goodness, and joy.

Galatians 5:22

Don't let _____ become weary in doing good but be alert to opportunities to show kindness and compassion to all people—especially to those who belong to the family of believers.

Galatians 6:9–10

Give _____ an undivided heart and a new spirit. Take away any hard and stony attitudes and replace them with a heart of flesh.

Ezekiel 11:19

May _____ live in harmony with siblings and friends and be sympathetic, compassionate, and humble toward everyone.

1 Peter 3:8

Anoint _____, as you anointed Jesus, to do good and bring your help and healing touch to others.

Acts 10:38

Let _____ show mercy and compassion to others, especially to orphans, foreigners, poor people, and others in great need.

Zechariah 7:9–10

Part 3

Praying for Your Teen's Health and Safety

Chapter 11

Praying for Your Teen Driver

He will command his angels concerning you
to guard you in all your ways.
Psalm 91:11

When our daughter Hillary got her driver's license, one of her friends—who had clipped a mailbox early in his driving career—said he'd give her twenty bucks if she could go a whole month without hitting anything. I quickly realized that my parental admonitions to "be careful!" were nothing compared to the satisfaction Hillary would get out of looting her friend, and when the first month passed without incident, I thought about slipping the guy another twenty to see if he could get her to go double or nothing. I'd read the reports about distracted driving—how texting while driving is six times more dangerous than drunk driving, for instance—and I wanted my girl to stay *focused*![1]

Teens and cars—like teens and almost anything that runs on gas or electricity—can be an unsettling mix. Sometimes the end result is aggravating, like the burn mark on the bathroom counter from the hair straightener that was left on all day, or the broken window that failed to survive the rocket-launcher science project. Sometimes it's a little bit funny, like the time one of my husband's relatives tried to unclog a toilet by using a cherry bomb (don't try it), or the time my girlfriend's daughter closed her eyes while piloting a motor scooter so she could "feel the breeze in her face and the wind in her hair"—and wound up feeling a mailbox. And sometimes it turns into a parent's worst nightmare. I'm not the weepy sort, but I still can't hear my friend Anne tell her story without reaching for a tissue . . .

Anne grabbed a half-finished Gatorade and shoved the bottle into the trash bag she was holding. With all four of her children involved in multiple sports, she sometimes felt like her car was a locker room. She pulled out a sock from under one of the seats, grateful for a sunny Saturday and a moment's peace so she could get herself organized for the week ahead.

Fifteen minutes earlier, Anne had waved goodbye to her husband, Bob, and their oldest daughter, fifteen-year-old Peyton. Peyton had been driving with a learner's permit for a month, and when Bob said he wanted to catch up on some work at his office, Peyton had offered to drive him there. The ride would allow her to log some highway miles, and she figured she could use the weekend's quiet to study while her dad worked.

Anne could hear her seven-year-old son, Robert, playing basketball with a friend. Suddenly, another sound pierced the air: it was her cell phone, which she had—providentially—brought outside while she worked.

"Hello," she said, cradling the phone under one ear.

The voice on the other end was incoherent. It sounded like Peyton, but Anne couldn't make out her words. Whatever it was, something was terribly wrong.

"Peyton—calm down!" Anne cried out, her heart pounding. "Tell me what's wrong."

Peyton continued to scream, her words coming fast and on top of each other. A few words suddenly cut through the jumble: *"I killed Daddy! I killed Daddy!"*

Anne's vision blurred. She knew she was going to faint. And then, in an instant, she felt calm and detached—like this horrible drama was unfolding in another world, happening to someone she did not know.

"Peyton, please calm down," Anne repeated. "Catch your breath."

It was as though her daughter had not heard. Peyton continued to wail. Finally another voice came on the phone—one that Anne did not recognize. "Your husband and your daughter have been in an accident," the woman said. "Your daughter is fine, and the rescue workers are with your husband right now."

Adrenaline took over. Hardly knowing what she was doing, Anne grabbed Robert and his friend, pushed them into the car, and began driving. "Jesus, save my husband!" she cried, over and over again. "Please, Jesus! Save him!"

When she reached the highway, all of the lanes were clogged. Seeing rescue lights in the distance, Anne steered her car into the emergency lane and sped forward. She got as close as she could, and then, telling the boys to stay put, she jumped out of the car. A fireman approached.

"Tell me the truth!" Anne begged. "What happened to my husband?"

"He's alive," the man said, "but they're taking him to the hospital. The car flipped three times."

Anne's eyes searched the scene. She saw the ambulance, and then her white Suburban, its top crushed nearly flat and its windows completely gone. *No one*, she thought, *could have survived.* Suddenly, Peyton was there, crying hysterically.

"I'm so sorry, Mom. I'm so sorry!"

Anne hugged her daughter tightly and then released her into the arms of a stranger. She had to find Bob. Hurrying toward the ambulance, she could see a stretcher inside. She pushed past the crowd of medical workers and threw herself onto her husband. *"Please, Jesus! Please . . ."*

I met up with Anne later that day at the hospital. Bob was still in the emergency room. He had suffered a slight concussion, and the doctors were busy taking glass shards out of his head. Apart from that, he was fine. And aside from a few cuts on her legs, Peyton was unharmed as well.

"It's a miracle!" Anne said. "It's a miracle that they crossed three lanes of highway traffic and didn't hit any other cars. It's a miracle that they're alive! The man who pulled Peyton out of the car asked her if she believed in angels. He saw the whole thing happen—and he said that angels had saved her. I believe it."

I believed it too—particularly after Anne shared one of her favorite prayer verses with me. "Psalm 91," she said. "Especially

Praying for Your Teen Driver

verses 11 and 12, where it says that God will give his angels charge over you, to keep you in all your ways and bear you up, lest you dash your foot against a stone. I pray these verses pretty much every day for my family."

Psalm 91 ends with God's promise that when we acknowledge his name, we can call on him and know he will protect us and answer us. He promises to be with us in times of trouble and to deliver us (verses 14 and 15).

I remember speaking at a church in San Francisco, where I had been asked to talk about the power of praying the Scriptures. Afterward, an older gentleman approached. His eyes were bright blue, and they glistened with tears. "I was a teen when I served in World War II," he told me. "When I came home, my father showed me Psalm 91. He said he had prayed it for me every single day while I was gone."

That's how it is with God's Word. It never changes. A psalm that was written three thousand years ago is just as potent and applicable today as it was eighty years ago, when a young soldier fought in Europe, and as it was just a few years ago, when a young driver was on the highway. The power David recognized when he wrote Psalm 91 is the very same power we can tap into now. "The grass withers and the flowers fall, but the word of our God endures forever."[2]

PRAYER PRINCIPLE

When you pray the Scriptures, you tap
into the same power that has been
working in the lives of teens forever.

Poised for Prayer

In the same way, God himself does not change. James 1:17 says that "every good and perfect gift is from above, coming down from the Father of the heavenly lights, who does not change like shifting shadows." Safety and protection are gifts that all of us want for our children. When we ask God to give these gifts to our kids—whether they're in the car or anyplace else—we can do so knowing that he has a long history of keeping his eye on teens. He shut the lions' mouths for Daniel and shielded his friends from the scorching flames of the fiery furnace. He rescued a young Queen Esther from the genocidal schemes of her vile adversary. And he protected David, the boy armed only with a slingshot and a handful of stones, from the power and wrath of a giant.[3]

Sometimes I wish that the Bible gave us more insight into how the *parents* of some of these teens felt. When David's dad sent him to the battlefield, it was with instructions to bring some bread and cheese to his older brothers and to report back on how they were faring against the Philistines. I suspect he had no idea that the boy would drop off the meal and then decide to take on a giant! But isn't that always the way it is? Who can predict what a teen will do?

PRAYER PRINCIPLE

We can't predict what our teens will do, but
we can count on God to be with them.

The teen years show us, as perhaps never before, that our parental influence is limited. We are no longer in control. We cannot always be with our kids, and we don't always know who they're with—a lot of times, we aren't even sure where exactly they are. We can't be there to tell our teens how fast to drive, where to turn, or even what to say or do in any given situation—and even if we could do these things, would they listen? We can warn them, encourage them, teach them, and even threaten them, but at the end of the day, they are out of our reach.

But they are *never* out of God's reach. His arm, as he reminds us repeatedly, is never too short.[4]

When our kids come up against a rocky place—whether a sickness, an accident, or the consequence of a foolish decision (like putting a cherry bomb in a toilet)—God promises to be with them. I love how he puts it in Isaiah 43:2 (NLT):

> When you go through deep waters,
>   I will be with you.
> When you go through rivers of difficulty,
>   you will not drown.
> When you walk through the fire of oppression,
>   you will not be burned up;
>   the flames will not consume you.

Note that this verse does not say *if* you go through deep waters, but *when*. Trouble and difficulty and fiery trials are sure to come—and sometimes the teen years are where we find the deepest waters and the hottest fires. Our faith will be tested. But as we turn our kids over to the Lord, trusting in his long arm and his mighty presence, we can do so knowing that he will be with them.

And also with us.

Prayers You Can Use

Heavenly Father . . .

When _____ gets behind the wheel, guide them in the way of wisdom and lead them along straight paths.

Proverbs 4:11

Keep _____ in perfect peace on the road. Make the way smooth, and prompt _____ to follow your laws—including things like speed limits!   *Isaiah 26:3–8*

When disaster strikes—maybe in the form of a flat tire, an accident, or some other mishap—send your angels to encamp around _____ and bring comfort, protection, and healing.

Psalm 34:7; Hebrews 1:14

Help me release _____ to you when they get behind the wheel or in a friend's car, knowing that as I cast all my anxiety on you, you will care for them—and for me.   *1 Peter 5:7*

Watch over _____. By day and by night, protect them from all harm. Watch over their coming and going, now and always.

Psalm 121:3–8

When _____ faces difficulty on the road, like getting lost, being stuck in traffic jams, and so on, don't let them become frightened or dismayed. Be with _____ to bring strength and help.   *Isaiah 41:10*

Rescue _____ from every evil attack and danger, and bring them safely to your heavenly kingdom.

2 Timothy 4:18

Be _____'s shield. Guard their course and protect their way.

Proverbs 2:7–8

Don't let _____ drive like Jehu—like a maniac!

2 Kings 9:20

Don't let _____ be an anxious driver. Let them be self-controlled and alert to danger.

1 Peter 5:7–8

Keep _____ focused on wisdom and understanding, preserving sound judgment and discretion when they drive.

Proverbs 3:21

Help me know what rules and boundaries to establish for _____ when they drive, and prompt them to listen to my instruction and not forsake my teaching.

Proverbs 1:8

Command your angels concerning _____ to guard them in all their ways.

Psalm 91:11

Chapter 12

Praying for Healing from Eating Disorders and Negative Body Image

We are God's masterpiece.
Ephesians 2:10 NLT

Our daughter Annesley was a peer counselor at her school. Her job wasn't to fix people's problems or give advice; she was mainly supposed to be an available and willing listener. The school had a professional counselor on staff, as well as an extensive network of referral options, but the peer counseling program provided a confidential and nonthreatening entry point for students who needed help sorting through their options, with the hope that they'd be better equipped to solve their own problems.

Peer counselors receive training about all sorts of teen issues, from sexually transmitted diseases and teen pregnancy to drug abuse, self-harm, and suicide. When I asked Annesley which aspect of the training had been the most valuable, she didn't hesitate.

"Eating disorders," she said. "They gave us so much good information about the signs and causes and treatment options. Plus, out of all of the problems we covered, eating disorders were probably the most common."

Given the appearance-obsessed attitude of our culture, the increasing prevalence of eating disorders—including anorexia, bulimia, weight and body image disorder, excessive exercise, and orthorexia (a fixation on eating only "healthy" foods)—is understandable. Teen-oriented magazines that once offered articles like "Snag a Guy! Bake Him a Pie!" are now filled with weight-loss gimmicks and pictures of impossibly thin women in scanty clothing. And researchers have found that women who looked at these magazine photos showed greater signs of depression and were more dissatisfied with their bodies after only one to three minutes of viewing the pictures.[1]

Although eating and body image disorders affect both men and women from all ethnicities, ages, and socioeconomic backgrounds, the vast majority (90 percent) of people who suffer are women between the ages of twelve and twenty-five.[2] As I reviewed the research—noting the contributing factors (such things as social pressure to be thin, family stress, emotional insecurities, and a tendency toward perfectionism), as well as the accompanying medical problems (changes in brain size, bone and muscle mass, menstrual cycles, heart and liver functions, and a host of other scary stuff)—I found myself growing more and more discouraged. I thought about our own daughters and their precious friends, many of whom have bought into the lie that their self-worth is tied to the way they look. Rather than seeing themselves the way God does—as his "masterpiece"—they look in the mirror and see only their flaws.[3]

What can we say to encourage our daughters? How can we pray?

I shared these questions, along with my discouragement, with a mom named Debra, who gave me a reason to hope . . .

∼ ∼ ∼

"Mom, can I go for a run?"

"Olivia!" Debra replied, "It's ten o'clock! It's pitch-dark outside."

"I know, Mom, but I need a study break. Pleeeeease."

Teen girls! Debra shook her head, half wondering whether she would make it through Olivia's senior year. Even as she grumbled, though, she rummaged around for a sweater in the closet. If Olivia was going to go for a run, she wasn't going to go alone. Debra didn't intend to suit up; rather, she planned to stick her head out the door and keep watch.

"I'll tell you what," she offered. "You can run down to the Johnsons' house and back."

"Mom, that's just four houses away!"

"I know. You can go back and forth a hundred times if you want to. Take it or leave it."

Olivia took it—just as Debra knew she would. That girl could not go a day without some form of serious exercise.

As Olivia beat a path up and down their street, Debra found her thoughts running just as fast. Anyone would say that Olivia had a cute figure—all traces of her preadolescent pudginess had vanished—but she was definitely more than a little concerned about her weight. As a middle schooler, she had started packing her own lunches to ensure they weren't too fattening. By the time she hit high school, what began as a novelty had become an obsession. Debra would never forget the family vacation where Olivia's refusal to eat hot dogs and potato chips had transformed a low-key lunch into a tearful, angry scene.

Counseling helped, but Debra sensed that the therapists didn't really understand the underlying issues. They seemed more concerned with treating Olivia's physical symptoms than with helping her overcome any anxiety or emotional hurts she might have. Similarly, the medical community didn't appear to be overly worried about Olivia's health. At five feet seven inches tall and weighing just 106 pounds, Olivia was definitely thin, but a doctor had assured Debra that she was "okay." Debra wanted to believe he was right.

Now, as Olivia returned from her run, Debra found herself wondering what the future would hold. Olivia would soon be in college, and hard as it would be, Debra resolved not to become one of those overprotective mothers who called to check up on her child all the time. Rather, she wanted to let her little girl enjoy a taste of independence.

But a few months later, when Olivia came home for Thanksgiving and family members heard her throwing up in the bathroom, Debra knew she had a serious problem. Olivia had found yet another way—beyond limiting her food intake and exercising compulsively—to keep her weight down.

Always a praying mom, Debra redoubled her efforts. She prayed against the stronghold of vanity and of any obsessive-compulsive behaviors that may have taken root in Olivia's life. She asked God to renew Olivia's mind and transform her thoughts so she would see her body as something holy and pleasing to God.

And fearful that she might say the wrong thing as she tried to encourage her daughter, Debra asked God to put his words in her mouth—even as he kept them safe under the protection of his hand.[4]

PRAYER PRINCIPLE

In addition to asking God to help your teen, ask him to help you. Ask him to put his words in your mouth.

Things got better—and then worse. Olivia gained some weight and didn't balk at what she saw in the mirror. She still struggled with anxiety, though, and after a bout of depression and a breakup with a fellow she *thought* she was going to marry, she discovered she was pregnant.

Knowing she would keep her baby, Olivia took a year off from school.

"Olivia had a great pregnancy," Debra says somewhat wryly. "She was amazingly fit, working out every day. We even stopped at a twenty-four-hour fitness center on the way to the hospital so she could get in one last workout before the baby came!"

Today, little Sarah is the light of Olivia's life—and the chief reason Olivia stopped starving herself. She finished her college degree and set her sights on becoming a registered dietician. "I want to help my daughter and other young girls learn to control their weight in a *healthy* way instead of taking the drastic measures I took," Olivia says.

For her part, Debra continues to pray—and babysit when Olivia wants to hit the gym. "Without the Lord," she says, "I probably would have thought, like the rest of the world, that Olivia would always have an eating disorder—either limiting her calories or overexercising to keep the weight off. But with God, all things are possible! He is the One who is renewing Olivia's mind. I am counting on him to completely deliver her—and when *he* is in control, and not the eating disorder, she will be a prisoner set free!"

PRAYER PRINCIPLE

Thank God for what he has done in your
teen's life—and believe for the answers
to prayer that are yet to come.

Poised for Prayer

I have to tell you that as I talked with Debra, I couldn't help myself. I *had* to ask the question. "Debra," I said, "you sound like an amazing mother. You seem so, so—*fine* about everything. If I had a daughter who asked me to stop at the gym when she was in labor, I think I might go a little bonkers. How can you be so *patient*?"

"Oh, goodness, I am definitely not patient!" Debra laughed. "I have been mad and scared and frustrated. I've cried buckets of tears, and Olivia and I have certainly had plenty of arguments—especially when I think she's making a bad choice or taking an unnecessary risk. I *still* struggle with whether to make a cake or not, or whether to tell Olivia she looks great when she says she's lost two pounds. I worry that I'll be too controlling or that I'll say the wrong thing.

"But I *do* trust God. I've asked him to put his words in my mouth, and I rely on his strength and wisdom every day. One of my favorite things to do is read my Bible and find Scriptures I can pray that match our specific needs—God's Word is just *so* important."

Obviously, I could not agree more. And if your teen is struggling with an eating disorder—or with anything that chips away at their sense of self-worth or their ability to see themselves through God's eyes—point them toward the transforming truth of his Word, both in your prayers and through what you say. Tell your daughter (and your son!) that they are "fearfully and wonderfully made" and that God created them just as they are. Remind them that, as they behold God's glory, they are being made more and more like him, reflecting his glorious image. God is enthralled by their beauty—ask him to help them believe that![5]

And above all, ask God to give your teen an identity that is rooted and built up in Jesus—one where their faith can grow strong and their heart overflows with thankfulness—and pray against anything that would take them captive with the hollow and deceptive philosophy that says our worth is defined by the way we look.[6]

As you pray, don't be afraid to seek professional advice. I cringed over the devastating symptoms and sometimes life-threatening medical complications that can accompany eating disorders, but I was encouraged to read about the treatment options, as well as the recovery rate for those who get help.

Like Debra, you may not always know what to do or what to say. But God does. As you pray for your teen, depend on God's faithfulness, his love, and his Word. As Debra would say, there's no better place to anchor your trust.

Prayers You Can Use

Heavenly Father . . .

Let _____ know that you made them and that all your ways are perfect. Nourish _____ as you nourished the Israelites, and keep them safe in your hand.

Deuteronomy 32:4, 6, 13, 39

When _____ is anxious, be their security and shield; let them rest between your shoulders. Lead _____ into a land of safety, a land where they can see the food and drink you provide as gifts rather than something to be feared or abused.

Deuteronomy 33:12, 28

Remind _____ that you do not look at the things human beings look at—such as outward appearance—but that you value what's in the heart.

1 Samuel 16:7

Cause _____ to hope in your unfailing love, and deliver them from death. Keep _____ alive, even during times of self-imposed famine.

Psalm 33:18–19

Protect _____ so that they will not be taken captive by the world's hollow and deceptive philosophy that attaches worth and value to appearance.

Colossians 2:8

Bring your peace to _____'s heart, because a heart at peace gives life to the body.

Proverbs 14:30

Let _____ feast on your Word. Let the words of Scripture be their joy and delight. *Jeremiah 15:16*

You are the God of peace. Please make _____ holy in every way, letting their whole spirit, soul, and body be kept blameless until Jesus comes again. *1 Thessalonians 5:23*

Direct _____'s thoughts so that they will be set on things above, not on earthly things, such weight or appearance. Help _____ put to death those things that belong to their earthly nature, including any obsession with appearance, which is a form of idolatry. *Colossians 3:2, 5*

When I speak to _____, help my words to be kind. Let them be like honey—sweet to the soul and healthy for the body. *Proverbs 16:24*

Set _____ free from the prison of a distorted self-image, that they may praise your name. *Psalm 142:7*

Bless _____ and keep them; make your face shine upon them. Be gracious to them, and give them peace. *Numbers 6:24–26*

Search _____ and know their thoughts. Place your hand of blessing and protection on _____. Let them know that they are fearfully and wonderfully made, and that when you look at them—as you have done since even before they were born—you see your beautiful handiwork. *Psalm 139:1, 5, 13–14*

When _____ loathes food and draws near death, save them from their distress.

Psalm 107:18–19

I pray that out of your glorious riches you will strengthen _____ with power through your Spirit in their inner being.

Ephesians 3:16

Demolish strongholds of vanity, insecurity, anxiety, and perfectionism in _____'s life.

2 Corinthians 10:4

Transform _____ by renewing their mind so that they can see themselves as you do.

Romans 12:1–2

Chapter 13

Praying against Self-Harm and Suicide

The LORD has chosen you to be his treasured possession.
Deuteronomy 14:2

I first heard about the practice of cutting when our oldest daughter was in middle school. We lived in southern California at the time, and a couple of girls in her grade had been seen with razor marks on their arms. My heart ached for the girls and their families. *What would make a teen want to hurt herself in that way?*

Back then, I thought the girls' behavior was an isolated incident, one of those "out there" things a kid growing up in the shadow of Hollywood might decide to try. Now, though, I know that adolescent self-harm, often through cutting and burning, is alarmingly common as teens struggle to cope with stress at school, in their families, and in peer relationships. And teen suicide—self-harm's evil cousin—is also on the rise, jumping 56 percent in a single decade. Today, suicide is the second leading cause of death among adolescents, right behind car wrecks and other accidents.[1]

Statistics like these would come as no surprise to my friend

Karen—nor would the findings that say that self-harm and suicidal thoughts cross racial, gender, and socioeconomic boundaries. To all appearances, Karen's daughter Natalie looked like she had a near-perfect teen life . . .

ॐ ॐ ॐ

Natalie hung up the phone, anger and hurt boiling inside her. She had tried to help her friend, to make her see that having sex with her boyfriend was not a good idea, but it was no use. Rachel didn't want to hear it, and their heated conversation had made one thing perfectly clear: not only was she rejecting Natalie's advice; she was rejecting her friendship.

Grabbing her tennis racquet, Natalie headed outside, slamming the door behind her. *Whack! Whack! Whack!* She smacked the ball against the garage door, over and over again, tears blurring her vision. She was just so *angry*! Stooping to pick up the ball, she felt as though she would explode. She slammed her fist into the stucco wall.

Her knuckles were ripped and bloody, but Natalie didn't care. Right now, she hated Rachel. She hated herself. Why had she even said anything? So much for the Bible's command to speak the truth in love.[2] When it came to friendships, speaking the truth could be far too costly.

Natalie went back inside, now more hurt than angry. She knew a couple of girls at school who had cut themselves, saying it gave them a sense of control. At first, Natalie had thought they were weird; now she wasn't so sure. Maybe they knew something she didn't.

Natalie opened the cabinet above her sink, searching for something sharp. Would a disposable razor work? She didn't know—and frankly, she didn't care. Right now, she just wanted to find an outlet for her pain. She drew the blade across the back of her hand and watched, transfixed, as the blood came. It hurt, but in a strange way it also felt like a release. She pressed the razor into her other hand.

The next morning, a series of angry red lines were all that remained of Natalie's rage. She managed to leave the house without anyone seeing the marks, but at school they weren't so easy to hide. A friend alerted the school counselor, who called Natalie into his office. That night she told her parents what she had done.

Karen was as stunned as she was confused. Natalie was a gifted athlete, the president of her sophomore class, and a leader in the church youth group. Not only that, but she was gorgeous. To look at her, no one would ever guess that anything could be wrong in her life!

Karen felt as though she had failed as a mother. "When I saw Natalie's hands," she told me, "all I could think about was that these were the same hands I kissed that day in the hospital when she was born. They were the hands that had slipped into mine when she was a little girl, as the two of us looked for shells on the beach. They were beautiful hands—and they still are; only now they look angry and scarred. What was going on inside my baby girl? Why would she want to hurt herself?"

Karen and Tom cried out to God for wisdom and insight. They also reached out to a professional counselor for advice.

The counselor helped them understand some of the things

that might be going on in Natalie's mind, like how even something like a desire for good grades or being popular with her friends can create unimaginable stress for a teen who thinks she needs to do everything "right." Equipped with a new perspective on how they could help their daughter, Karen and Tom asked God to show them what they could do.

God answered that prayer—but not in the way they expected. Instead of telling them what to do, God revealed what he had already done.

"The main way that God speaks to me is through Scripture," Karen said, "and as I was praying for Natalie, I came across Isaiah 49:15. Here's what it says: 'Can a mother forget the baby at her breast and have no compassion on the child she has borne? Though she may forget, I will not forget you!' When I read those words, I knew that God was speaking to me, saying that he loves Natalie and that he will never forget her. He has everything under control."

"But," she continued, "that's not the best part. The best part is verse 16, where God says, 'I have engraved you on the palms of my hands.'"

I have engraved you on the palms of my hands.

"I know that Natalie's hands were marked by anger," Karen said softly. "But God's hands are marked by love. He has Natalie's name written on his hands. I can trust him to take care of her."

PRAYER PRINCIPLE

God will never forget your child. Their name
is engraved on the palms of his hands.

Karen and Tom continued to pray, asking God to bring

good out of Natalie's pain. One night, several weeks later, Karen slipped into Natalie's room to kiss her good night. She found her daughter propped up in bed, an open Bible on her lap.

"Hey, Mom," Natalie said, "do you know what it says in James 1:2?"

"Tell me," Karen prompted.

"It says we're supposed to consider it pure joy whenever we face trials, because God uses them to test our faith and make us complete. I've had a lot of trials this year—"

"Uh-huh," Karen agreed, waiting for her daughter to continue.

"So I guess it's all good. I mean, God is going to use the bad stuff to bring about good stuff. And that promise gives me joy."

Karen wanted to say something, but her emotion choked her words. Through one simple verse, God had answered her prayer for redemption. He had filled her daughter's heart with joy and with a few simple words opened the door to hope. Karen knew the road ahead could still be rocky (and that Natalie could still put undue pressure on herself), but God had shown himself faithful. Having begun a good work, he could be counted on to complete it.[3]

Poised for Prayer

When Karen told me her story, she said one of the hardest things for her was that she felt so ill-equipped to help her daughter. We get that, don't we? When teens struggle—whether the problem involves self-injury, peer relationships, suicide attempts, or something else—there are plenty of times when parents don't understand what is happening, and we don't always know how to help. Many times, we aren't even sure how to pray.

The good news is that God knew there'd be days—and even entire seasons—like that. During those uncertain times, we can turn to the Holy Spirit for help. I love how Romans 8:26 reads in the NLT: "The Holy Spirit helps us in our weakness. For example, we don't know what God wants us to pray for. But the Holy Spirit prays for us with groanings that cannot be expressed in words."

PRAYER PRINCIPLE

The Holy Spirit helps us when we
don't know how to pray.

The God who searches our hearts and those of our teens knows exactly what is needed. As parents, we can turn to him in our greatest weakness and confusion, knowing that not only will his Spirit *help* us, but that he will *pray* for us—and that even in the most bewildering or painful challenges, he will cause everything to work together for the good of those who love God and are called according to his purpose for them.[4]

Like you, I want God's best for my kids. As I reflect on these verses, I cannot imagine a greater privilege than that of joining our human hearts and longings together with the mind of the Holy Spirit, trusting in the power of prayer as we ask God to place his protective arms around our teens and accomplish his beautiful purposes in their lives.

Their names are ever before him, written on his palms as his Spirit prays.

Prayers You Can Use

Heavenly Father . . .

Make known to _____ the path of life; fill them with joy in your presence.   *Psalm 16:11*

Protect _____ from the thief who comes only to steal and kill and destroy; give _____ life—life to the full.

John 10:10

Make _____ holy in every way—in spirit, soul, and body.
1 Thessalonians 5:23 NLT

Let _____ take refuge in you and be glad; let them ever sing for joy. Spread your protection over _____ that they may rejoice in you.   *Psalm 5:11*

Remind _____ that they belong to you. May _____ rest in your presence, safe from the condemnation of their own heart.
1 John 3:19–20

Keep _____ from all harm. Watch over their life—their coming and going—both now and forevermore.

Psalm 121:7–8

May _____'s identity be firmly rooted and established in Christ's love. Give _____ the power to grasp how wide and long and high and deep your love is for them.

Ephesians 3:17–18

You have kept track of _____'s sorrows, collecting their tears in a bottle. Prompt _____ to call on you for help, confident that you are on their side. *Psalm 56:8–9*

Let _____ know that they are your special possession. Call _____ out of darkness into your wonderful light.

1 Peter 2:9

Whatever is true, whatever is noble, whatever is right, whatever is pure, whatever is lovely, whatever is admirable—if anything is excellent or praiseworthy—cause _____ to think about such things. *Philippians 4:8*

Help _____ remember that their body is a temple where the Holy Spirit lives. Remind _____ that they belong to you and should honor you with their body.

1 Corinthians 6:19–20

Show _____ that even if it seems as though everyone has forgotten or neglected them, you never will. Let them know that their name is engraved on the palms of your hands.

Isaiah 49:15–16

Let _____ find joy in even the most painful circumstances, knowing that you use trials to develop endurance, strengthen character, and make us mature and complete, not lacking anything.   *James 1:2–4*

When _____ has to choose between life and death, blessings and curses, prompt them to choose life so that they and their children may live.   *Deuteronomy 30:19*

Turn_____ back from the pit, that the light of life may shine on them.   *Job 33:30*

Keep _____ from cutting or harming themselves in any way, since they are your children, your treasured possession.
                                                                                          Deuteronomy 14:1–2

Chapter 14

Praying through Anxiety and Depression

Bestow on them a crown of beauty
  instead of ashes,
the oil of joy
  instead of mourning,
and a garment of praise
  instead of a spirit of despair.
Isaiah 61:3

When my father had the blues, he used to say that he felt "lower than whale vomit." Whale vomit, he told me, sinks to the bottom of the ocean; in other words, it's down about as far as you can get.

I'm no marine biologist, and I can't vouch for the accuracy of my dad's claims, but I'm guessing Jonah knew a little something about the subject. Shortly after the big fish barfed him onto the beach, Jonah found himself in a full-scale pout—but it wasn't because of the whale. Jonah was miffed that God hadn't wiped out the city of Nineveh like Jonah had warned he would. "Just kill me now, LORD!" he said. "I'd rather be dead than alive if what I predicted will not happen."[1]

Jonah is just one of the Bible's many moaners and groaners. Check out David's complaint: "My bones are weak; my body is tired; and even my soul is exhausted. My neighbors don't like me, and my friends have forgotten me—it's like they think I'm as useless as a broken dish." Or how about Naomi, Ruth's mother-in-law: "Don't call me 'Pleasant'; call me 'Bitter,' because that's my life." Or the prophet Elijah, the fellow who called down fire from heaven, did away with nine hundred false prophets, outran a chariot with his cloak tucked into his belt, and then, exhausted and alone, plopped down under a tree and went to sleep. "I've had enough," he said—and he prayed that God would end his life.[2]

I don't know about you, but I take a sort of perverse "misery loves company" pleasure in knowing that God's people—his *Bible* people—knew what it was like to wrestle with fear, loneliness, exhaustion, disappointment, bitterness, anxiety, grief, and depression. Even so, it can be tough when these difficult emotions weasel their way into our lives—and even harder when they leap onto the backs of our teens.

Sometimes the problems can be hard to spot. My friend Paula thought her daughter Lily had finally hit her stride when she transitioned from high school to college. She had made plenty of friends, earned excellent grades, landed a part-time job in her field of study, and—best of all, perhaps—she'd lost the last of the baby fat she'd still carried in high school. To Paula's eye, her daughter looked healthy and fit—and she was stunned when Lily came home after her freshman year and confessed to experiencing an anxiety so fierce that, most days, she worried that she was having a heart attack.

"And there I was," Paula said, "feeling so proud of my girl for all she had accomplished. I had no idea how much pressure she was putting on herself to perform!"

My friend Camille, on the other hand, had no trouble recognizing that something was troubling her daughter, Hailey. She just didn't realize how serious the problem was. . .

୭ ୭ ୭

Camille picked up the potato chip bag and dropped into the recycle bin the soda can she had found next to the television set. She wanted to chastise Hailey, but she bit her tongue. Teens were supposed to be slobs and eat junk food, right? It wasn't Hailey's fault that she happened to be born into a household that included a neatnik mother.

When she noticed the lump on the couch, however, Camille decided to speak up. "Hey, Hails," she said, patting the blanket. "Why don't you get up and go for a run? Or go out and shoot some baskets. It's a beautiful day—and you know what Coach Higgins said. You all are supposed to be working out on the weekends."

"Maybe later," Hailey mumbled, pulling the cover over her head. "I'm too tired right now."

Camille was glad Hailey couldn't see her face. She was worried—very much so. A year ago, Hailey's academic performance had started to slip. Normally an honor student, she had brought home a disappointing report card, and one of the teachers had observed that Hailey had seemed to have "lost interest" in her schoolwork. Not only that, but Hailey had also lost interest in her friends. When they called or dropped by, Hailey often responded with indifference or apathy. Camille didn't think the teens would put up with that sort of reception much longer; she worried that Hailey would wind up alone.

Knowing that her own fear and anxiety wouldn't help matters, Camille took her concerns to God.

"Lord," she prayed, "my heart is breaking for my precious daughter. She seems so sad and lonely; I just don't know what to do."

Two days later, Camille sensed God speaking as she read her Bible. The words of Deuteronomy 20:3–4, originally given to the Israelites as they prepared for battle, seemed to jump off the page: "Do not be fainthearted or afraid; do not panic or be terrified by them. For the LORD your God is the one who goes with you to fight for you against your enemies to give you victory."

I know the problem looks huge, God whispered to Camille's heart, *but don't be afraid. Don't panic. Just get out of the way, and let me fight the battle.*

PRAYER PRINCIPLE

God will fight for your teen. And he'll fight for you.

Encouraged by those words, Camille resolved to quit nagging—and to keep praying. At the same time, she and her husband, Sam, had read about the signs of depression—things like an inability to concentrate, declining academic performance, a loss of friends, increased fatigue, and mood swings—and they decided it would be prudent to meet with a professional counselor.

"Hailey is definitely minimizing things in her life," the woman said when they met privately after she had talked with Hailey. "Is there any family history of depression?"

Camille felt her heart skip a beat. Both her mother and Sam's mother had been treated for depression, but they had discounted any possible connection to Hailey's situation, figuring that an older woman's problems were nothing like what a teen might be going through.

"I'm not overly concerned," the counselor said, "but I definitely see signs of mild depression. Let's see how things go—and please don't hesitate to call if you need me."

The ensuing months were difficult ones. Hailey seemed to take two steps forward and one step back, and each time Camille and Sam thought she had turned a corner, something would happen—a fight with a friend, an outburst of aggression, a quiet descent into sullenness. Camille desperately wanted to do something to "fix" Hailey's problems, and she hated feeling so helpless. Rather than dwelling on her limitations, though, she decided to focus on God's power and his love. She knew the words of 1 Peter 5:7 by heart—that God invited her to cast all her anxieties on him because he cared for her—and she figured she may as well take him up on his offer.

Camille found herself looking forward to her weekly Moms in Prayer meeting. She loved praying with the other moms and relished the Scripture verses they shared. More often than not, a particular verse seemed to be written especially for her. On one of Camille's darkest days—she was running late because she had been crying over one of Hailey's outbursts—she slipped into the meeting and arrived just in time to hear one of the women quote

Isaiah 46:4: "I have made you and I will carry you; I will sustain you and I will rescue you."

That's what Hailey needs, Camille thought to herself—*someone to rescue her; and that's what I need too—someone to carry me.*

Time passed, and Hailey seemed—slowly but surely—to be gaining confidence. She made some new friends at church, and as she prepared to go on a retreat with this group, Camille came across a verse that reflected the cry of her heart: "Give us gladness in proportion to our former misery! Replace the evil years with good. Let us, your servants, see you work again; let our children see your glory."[3]

"Things have definitely improved," Camille told me when I asked how Hailey was doing. "Her grades are up; she enjoys sports again and seems to have made some new friends. But I'm still praying the verse from Psalm 90 about proportionate gladness. If God is going to give us gladness in proportion to our former misery, then we definitely have some good years ahead!

"I hate to admit it," she continued, "but I think that God is using Hailey's struggles to teach me that I cannot fix everything and that I need to depend on him to work out his will in her life. It's a tough place to be, but I'm learning—slowly—that it's exactly where God wants me."

PRAYER PRINCIPLE

Our struggles are often God's entry points
as he invites us to depend on his power.

Poised for Prayer

My father—the one with the whale vomit wisdom—went to be with the Lord in 2001 after a yearlong bout with cancer. Five years later, my mother married a widower named John, a godly man I have come to deeply love and respect. When I told him I was working on this book, he shared a story that brought tears to my eyes.

"When I was about twelve years old," John said, "my mother came down with a crippling form of arthritis. Within a year, she was confined to her bed, and I grew up having to change her sheets and do almost everything for her. She never went to any of my school plays or sports events, never helped me with my homework, and couldn't even make a peanut butter and jelly sandwich to put in my lunch.

"The only thing my mother could do was pray. She prayed for me every day—and I knew it. And when I got older and had an opportunity to make some very ungodly decisions, I found I couldn't do it. I couldn't get away from my mother's prayers and from the memory of what she had done for me day after day, year after year—talking to God as she lay in her bed."

Whether you find yourself impaired by illness or—like my friend Camille—by circumstances that have left you unable to "fix" your teen's problems, don't despair. When you are in a position where all you can do is pray, you are in a powerful place indeed.

Earlier, I mentioned David, Naomi, and Elijah. These folks struggled with discouragement and depression—but that's only part of their story. In each instance, God wasn't finished with them yet. They cried out to him in the depths of despair, and he put them back on their feet.

In Elijah's case, God ministered to him with rest—and with some much-needed food and drink—before giving him a new mission.

For Naomi, bitterness gave way to joy as she waited on God to alter her lot in life, which he did—providing Ruth to walk alongside her and Boaz to provide for her—in a beautiful story of faithfulness and redemption.

And for David, the change took place as David adjusted his perspective, focusing less on his problems and more on God's unfailing love and protection. Out of the depths of his discouragement, David summoned his resolve and began to praise God. If you read his song recorded in Psalm 31, you'll see a man who went from anguish and sorrow to one who could say, with confidence and joy, "How abundant are the good things that you have stored up for those who fear you . . . Be strong and take heart, all you who hope in the LORD."[4]

Like Elijah, your teen may simply need rest and nourishment. Like Naomi, you may find yourself having to depend on other people—friends and counselors—to be God's arms as he works behind the scenes. Or like David, you (and, for that matter, your teen) may need to shift your focus from problems to praise.

Whatever your circumstance, know that the Lord hears your prayers. Be strong and take heart, and put your hope in the Lord.

He will make a way.

Prayers You Can Use

Heavenly Father . . .

When _____ is brokenhearted, bring healing and bind up
their wounds.   *Psalm 147:3*

Give _____ beauty for ashes, joy instead of mourning, and
praise instead of despair. Make _____ an oak of righteous-
ness, displaying your splendor.   *Isaiah 61:3*

Lift _____ out of the slimy pit, out of the mud and mire. Give
_____ a firm place to stand and a new song to sing—a hymn
of praise to you.   *Psalm 40:2–3*

Grant confidence to _____; let them see your goodness in
the land of the living. Equip _____ to be strong and take
heart as they wait for you.   *Psalm 27:13–14*

Remind _____ that no matter where they go or how low they
sink, your presence is there, and even the darkness is not dark to
you, for darkness is as light to you.   *Psalm 139:7–12*

When anxiety is great within _____, may your consolation
bring joy.   *Psalm 94:19*

Remind _____ that Jesus was despised and rejected by
others, and that he was a man of suffering, and familiar with pain.
                                                                  Isaiah 53:3

Prompt _____ to cast all their cares and anxieties on you because you care for them.   *1 Peter 5:7*

When _____ is in the depths of despair, be attentive to their cry for mercy and bring full redemption from anxiety, depression, or any other concern.   *Psalm 130:1-7*

Don't let _____ struggle under the weight of any burden, but cause them to come to you and find rest.

Matthew 11:28-30

When _____ is downcast and disturbed, prompt them to put their hope in you. Direct _____ with your love by day, and sing over them in the night.   *Psalm 42:5-8*

Don't let _____ be anxious about anything, but in every situation, by prayer and petition, with thanksgiving, may they present their requests to you. And may your peace, which transcends all understanding, guard their hearts and their minds in Christ Jesus.   *Philippians 4:6-7*

Satisfy _____ in the morning with your unfailing love, that they may sing for joy and be glad. Give _____ gladness for as many years as they have seen trouble.

Psalm 90:14-15

Do not let _____ be enslaved by depression or negative emotions, but enable them to stand firm in the freedom of Christ.

Galatians 5:1

Let the light of your face shine on _____. Fill their heart with joy, and let them lie down and sleep in peace.

Psalm 4:6–8

Cause _____ to obey your commands and remain in your love so they will be filled with complete joy. Let _____ delight in the security of your friendship, knowing that you have chosen them to impact the world by bearing fruit—fruit that will last.

John 15:10–16

Chapter 15

Praying for Your Teen Rebel

"My wayward children," says the LORD,
  "come back to me, and I will heal your wayward
    hearts."

Jeremiah 3:22 NLT

"Don't talk to your kids about God as much as you talk to God about your kids."

I forget where I first heard that line, but it's one of my favorite pieces of parenting wisdom, particularly during those seasons when our kids don't particularly want to hear us talk—about God, or about anything else.

Teens are not alone, of course, in their willingness to wander—to want to figure things out on their own, even when doing so takes them down a dangerous or disobedient path. "We all," the Bible says, "have gone astray, each of us has turned to our own way."[1] For a parent, though, it can be painful—and scary—to watch a child make choices that run counter to God's design, to the "rich and satisfying life" that Jesus says he wants us to enjoy.[2]

PRAYER PRINCIPLE

The most effective way to get your teens
to make good choices isn't to talk to them
about God; it's to talk to God about them.

When I started doing the research for this book, I reached out to a network of friends—and friends of friends—to ask people if they'd be willing to share their stories. I wanted to know how other Christian parents were navigating the sometimes-tricky teen years and, even more than that, I wanted to know how they were praying.

I'll never forget opening an email from a woman named Lara, a lifelong churchgoer who loved God and believed his Word to be true, but who had never considered using the Bible to help shape her prayers . . .

ॐ ॐ ॐ

Lara's world was spinning out of control. Her daughter Samantha was gone—and the nightmare was starting again.

Her mind flashed back to the first time Sam had run away, during the summer before her freshman year in high school. A tip from one of Sam's friends led Lara and her husband, Peter, to call the police, who found Samantha in a house where other young runaways were known to have stopped for shelter. The satanic symbols that marked the walls served as a chilling portent of the home's darker purpose: it served as a gateway to the streets of Los Angeles—and to prostitution.

At the time, Lara had been frantic—and then grateful beyond words that her daughter had been found so quickly. That very day, she and Peter had taken Sam to a counselor, who recommended that she be hospitalized for treatment of depression and low self-esteem. Lara and Peter were stunned: Samantha was a popular, straight-A student. She was athletic, musically talented, and pretty. Listening to the counselor's diagnosis, Lara had felt her heart sink. She didn't even know how much she didn't know about what was going on inside her precious daughter.

After a month at the treatment center, Sam had come home. The family celebrated her return, and Lara—who had spent her adult life in church and Bible study—had been thrilled by the news that Samantha had recommitted her life to Christ. At last, Lara's dream of having a healthy Christian family seemed within reach.

She and Peter had been fairly strict in the past, fearing that—if things were left up to her—Samantha would make hurtful and potentially life-scarring choices. *Maybe*, they had thought, *it was time to give her some more freedom.* But that was easier said than done, particularly when the "friends" who tended to gravitate into Samantha's orbit seemed to be such a troubled, rebellious lot. Trying to talk things out with Samantha rarely helped; more often than not, their conversations turned into arguments.

Now, looking at the empty bed in Samantha's room, Lara couldn't help but wonder whether they had given her too much freedom. It was the spring of Samantha's junior year—more than two years since the police had brought her home the first time—and she was gone again.

Lara felt like a total failure. Her only consolation was that, unlike the first time she had left, Samantha did not appear to be in imminent danger this time. Taking shelter with whatever school chum would have her (and sometimes sneaking into her boyfriend's house after dark), Samantha showed up for school, continued to get excellent grades, never missed a day of work at her after-school job, and even went to her piano lessons. The only thing she refused to do was to come home.

Knowing her daughter was nearby did little to ease Lara's pain. What should she and Peter do? Samantha was like a toddler, Lara thought, throwing a temper tantrum whenever the rules got in the way of her desire for independence. If they forced Samantha to come home, she would only run away again.

Lara decided to confide in a few close friends. After hearing what she was going through, one of them mentioned that she had heard about Moms in Prayer on the radio. Praying for their children couldn't hurt; in fact, Lara thought it would be a definite step in the right direction, particularly if she had other mothers who were willing to come alongside to give her strength. Even with Peter sharing the load, her burden had gotten too heavy to bear. Talking to God sounded like a relief.

The women began meeting weekly to pray. It didn't take long before Lara realized something was different. A lifelong Christian, she had always believed in prayer, but when this group of moms prayed, they often used Scripture—the actual words in the Bible—as the basis for their prayers, and for the first time, Lara began to sense that God's Word was alive. She couldn't seem to get enough of it. Even when she wasn't praying with the group, she found herself turning to her Bible, letting the words slip off the pages and into her heart to fill her with strength (Lara's prayers are in italics after the Bible quotations):

In my distress I called to the LORD;
    I cried to my God for help.
From his temple he heard my voice;
    my cry came before him . . .
He reached down from on high and took hold of me;
    he drew me out of deep waters.
He rescued me from my powerful enemy,
    from my foes, who were too strong for me.
They confronted me in the day of my disaster,
    but the LORD was my support.

Psalm 18:6, 16–18

Lord, help us. Rescue me. Rescue Samantha. Be our support.

Gently instruct those who oppose the truth. Perhaps God will change those people's hearts, and they will learn the truth. Then they will come to their senses and escape from the devil's trap. For they have been held captive by him to do whatever he wants.

2 Timothy 2:25–26 NLT

Teach me, Father, how to reach out to Samantha. Give her a knowledge of your truth, and let her escape Satan's trap.

When I am afraid, I put my trust in you.
    In God, whose word I praise—

Psalm 56:3–4

I do trust you, Lord. I do.

And then there were passages that seemed to be written expressly for Samantha. Lara hung on these words—praying the Scriptures when it was too painful to pray about the details of her daughter's life—and clung to the hope they provided:

"I will . . . recapture the hearts of the people of Israel, who have all deserted me for their idols."

Ezekiel 14:5

Recapture Samantha's heart, Almighty God, and let her return to you!

For the grace of God that offers salvation . . . teaches us to say "No" to ungodliness and worldly passions, and to live self-controlled, upright and godly lives in this present age.

Titus 2:11–12

Shed your grace on her, Lord. Teach her to say no to her worldly passions and desires and yes to the life you desire.

If you, LORD, kept a record of sins,
    Lord, who could stand?
But with you there is forgiveness,
    so that we can, with reverence, serve you.

I wait for the LORD, my whole being waits,
    and in his word I put my hope . . .
Put your hope in the LORD,

for with the LORD is unfailing love,
and with him is full redemption.

Psalm 130:3–5, 7

Thank you, Lord, that you do not keep a record of Samantha's sin—or of mine. My hope is in your word. Let Samantha's life—all of our lives—be fully redeemed by your unfailing love.

Five weeks after she had left, Samantha came home.

This time, there was no big celebration—and no dramatic, overnight change. With help from their pastor, Peter and Lara made a covenant with their daughter, a contract that outlined rules and freedoms that came with family life. Samantha agreed to continue in counseling, and Lara continued to pray. God, she knew, had protected Samantha when she and Peter could not; truly, as the psalmist said, God had "reached down from on high" and rescued their family.[3]

Today—more than two decades later—Samantha is still a risk taker. She often finds herself in prison and in other dangerous places, only she isn't running anymore. Instead, equipped with a PhD in clinical psychology, she is ministering to those who have found themselves scarred by wrong choices, people whom others have given up trying to help. She loves her family and treats them with appreciation and respect.

"It is so faith-building," Lara says, "to realize that God *was* at work, even when we couldn't see him. He is a faithful, powerful, redeeming God—and without him, we would never have made it through those dark years."

Poised for Prayer

All of the prayer concerns in this book are spiritual battlegrounds, but rebellion is an issue where Satan's hand is often the easiest to see. As the one who comes to "steal and kill and destroy,"[4] he likes nothing more than to rip our families apart, making parents and teens think their fight is with each other rather than with him.

PRAYER PRINCIPLE

As you fight for your teen in prayer, remember that the battle is not with your child; it's with the thief who comes to steal and kill and destroy.

Lara would be the first to tell you it isn't easy, but that perseverance—in pursuing your teen, in showing love when it's hard, and in prayer—is the key to winning this battle. Here's what I mean:

Pursue. Your teen may say they don't want to talk to you and don't want to do anything with you, but don't close the door on those things. Instead, do everything *you* can do to show you are interested in their life. Attend sports events and recitals; take them out to breakfast or lunch; ask about their friends, their schoolwork, their activities. If they rebuff you, don't be discouraged. Take your cues from Hebrews 10:

- stand your ground in the face of suffering, even when you are publicly exposed to insult and persecution (verses 32–33);
- do not throw away your confidence (verse 35);

- persevere, knowing that when you have done the will of God, you will receive what he has promised (verse 36).

Love. We often think of love as a warm and fuzzy feeling, but more often than not, love is a decision—one motivated by patience, kindness, perseverance, and hope.[5] Prodigal teens can be tough to love. And if we had to rely on our own strength, we would be doomed. Thankfully, though, we are not alone. God shows us what unconditional love looks like—he stays by our side and calls us back to him, no matter how often we blow it—and when we struggle to do the same thing for our kids, we can ask him to do it through us. We can be, as Scripture says, his "ambassadors" carrying Christ's love to our kids even as we plead with them to "come back to God."[6]

Pray. Lara saturated her heart and her mind with the promises in God's Word, praying "continually"—and we can do the same thing.[7] Set aside time each day when you and your spouse will commit to earnest prayer for your teen. If you're a single parent or if your spouse won't join you in prayer, ask God to give you another prayer partner. Take courage from Jesus' words in Matthew 18:19–20: "If two of you on earth agree about anything they ask for, it will be done for them by my Father in heaven. For where two or three gather in my name, there am I with them."

Because again, talking our kids about God is not nearly as important—or as effective—as talking to God about our kids.

Prayers You Can Use

Heavenly Father . . .

You know what it's like to teach a child to walk, to lead them with ties of love, and to bend down and feed them. Now, as _____ seems determined to turn from you, have compassion and do not be angry. Put an end to their rebellious plans, prompt them to follow you, and bring them home.   *Hosea 11:1–11*

Lift _____ out of the slimy pit, out of the mud and mire. Give _____ a firm place to stand and a new song to sing, a hymn of praise to you. May all who seek to harm _____ be turned back in confusion and disgrace.   *Psalm 40:2–3, 14*

Teach _____ to fear you and worship you and listen to your voice. Do not let them rebel against your commands, but cause them to follow you, so that all will be well.   *1 Samuel 12:14*

Bring people into _____'s life who will gently instruct them. Grant repentance leading to the knowledge of the truth, so that they will come to their senses and escape the trap of the devil, who has taken them captive to do his will.

2 Timothy 2:25–26

Let _____ listen to your voice. Do not let them harden their heart in rebellion, but put people in _____'s life who will bring encouragement so that they won't be hardened by sin's deceitfulness.   *Hebrews 3:7–13*

Save, help, and deliver _____ according to your great love. Give our family the help we need; with you, we will gain the victory as you trample our enemies.   *Psalm 108:6, 12–13*

Children are a reward from you. You compare them to arrows in a quiver. Help me point _____ straight toward you, and don't let us be put to shame by the people and forces who oppose us.
Psalm 127:3–5

Teach _____ to say no to ungodliness and worldly passions and live a self-controlled, upright, and godly life.
Titus 2:12

When _____ wanders in wastelands, sits in darkness as a prisoner in chains, or makes foolish and rebellious decisions that lead to affliction, may they cry out to you. Send out your word and heal _____; rescue them from the grave.
Psalm 107:4–20

Cause _____ to grab hold of wisdom and enjoy your protection. Do not let _____ set foot on the path of the wicked or walk in the way of evildoers, but instead lead them to walk in the path of the righteous.   *Proverbs 4:6, 14, 18*

Let _____ put their hope in your unfailing love, knowing that with you is full redemption from every kind of sin.
Psalm 130:7–8

Call _____ back to you, and heal their wayward heart.
Jeremiah 3:22 NLT

Thank you, Lord, for the riches of your kindness, forbearance, and patience. In your kindness, lead _____ toward repentance.

Romans 2:4

Even as the shepherd rejoiced in the return of his lost sheep, and the woman rejoiced when she found her lost coin, let us rejoice in your faithfulness when you bring _____ back to our home. Let the dead be made alive and the lost be found.

Luke 15:1–10, 32

Break down every proud argument against God and every wall in _____'s life that keeps them from finding God. Capture rebels, including _____, to bring them back to God and change them into people whose hearts' desire is obedience to Christ.

2 Corinthians 10:4–5 TLB

Turn _____ from darkness to light, from the power of Satan to God, that they may receive forgiveness of sins and a place among those who are sanctified by faith.

Acts 26:18

Part 4

Praying for Your Teen's Victory over Temptation

Chapter 16

Praying about Technology and Social Media

I will not set before my eyes
anything that is worthless.
Psalm 101:3 ESV

When I began working on the first edition of this book in 2005, parents were concerned about this new thing called Myspace. It wasn't just the idea of online conversations that felt strange to us; our kids were using a whole new lexicon, and half the time we had no idea what they were talking about. We quickly learned that JK meant "just kidding," that LMK meant "let me know," and that LOL did not, in fact, mean "lots of love" (and shouldn't be used, as one unfortunate parent did, to convey sympathy about someone's dog dying).

But there were other, more nefarious acronyms. When my friends and I attended an internet safety and awareness seminar at our high school, we left with a dictionary's worth of new terms. Some were sexually suggestive (NIFOC apparently means "nude in front of computer"); some were invitations (LMIRL is "let's meet in real life"); and some were designed to keep adults in the dark (POS, for instance, signals that a parent is looking over a teen's shoulder).

A couple weeks after the seminar, my friend Beth pulled up one of her daughter Lexy's online texts and read "ALJSLKAGHFSL," an acronym that was not in our packet. Figuring she stumbled onto some new lingo, she set about decoding the letters: *All lovers just say . . . Any losers jump ship . . . Apples leave juice stains . . .*

Nothing made sense, and finally, concerned that Lexy could be involved in something truly sinister, Beth asked her other daughter, Hannah, what the strange letters meant. "I'm really worried about Lexy," she said. "Do you know what she's talking about?"

Hannah took one look at the computer screen and burst into laughter. "Mom!" she cackled. "Those letters don't mean anything! That's just the sort of thing we type when we're frustrated or when we don't know what to say. It's just random keys—like when you're talking to somebody and you say, 'Aaaarggghh!'"

JSAKLGHS . . . OIGLKSAJKLFH! No wonder we have a hard time keeping up with our teens!

Fast-forward fifteen years. Myspace has given way to Facebook, Instagram, Snapchat, YouTube, and a host of even newer apps we could not have dreamed of back when the other parents and I were decoding initials. Throw in the easy-everywhere access to the internet via smartphones (45 percent of teens say they are online "constantly," and 97 percent of them use at least one social media platform[1]), and it's easy to understand why technology is the number one reason parents say that raising teens today is more complicated (and difficult) than it was in the past.[2]

For all of its blessings—things like ready access to

information, easy and efficient communication, and the ability to build social and business networks—technology also scares us. It can leave parents feeling out of control or overwhelmed by the ever-rising tide of apps and devices. And we can't even count on other parents to have our backs as we're navigating new and unfamiliar waters. As author Andy Crouch notes, "Parents who set limits on their children's use of technology often experience intense peer pressure—from other parents!"[3]

Crouch wrote a book called *The Tech-Wise Family*. He acknowledges all of the problems associated with technology and, in particular, social media use: loss of sleep, increased anxiety, feelings of low self-esteem, heightened peer pressure and opportunities for cyberbullying, loneliness, and a significant link to depression, to name just a few.[4] But the number one technological concern parents have, he says, is the ready access to pornography.

And indeed, we are right to be concerned. Depending on which study you cite, the average age of a child's first exposure to pornography is somewhere between eight and eleven years old (with children as young as five years old being exposed). And only 32 percent of teens say that viewing porn is wrong (versus the 56 percent who maintain that "not recycling" is immoral.)[5] "If you have teenage children," Crouch writes, "whether boys or girls, it is likely that they have already been exposed to pornography and that they have sought it out."[6]

My friend Sharon would agree. With her kids enrolled in Christian school and actively involved in their church, she didn't think she would have to worry about things like passwords, search engines, and filters on their phones and laptops. But all it took was a passing glance at her son's computer screen to let Sharon know that the threat was real . . .

෨෮ ෨෮ ෨෮

"Hey, Kyle!" Sharon called out to her son, who seemed focused on the computer in front of him. "Dinner is in about fifteen minutes—how's the homework coming?"

"Fine," Kyle mumbled. "Okay."

Stepping back from the stove to where she had a clear view of the family's home office, Sharon peered around to see what Kyle was working on. It didn't look much like homework; in fact, she was pretty sure that what she was seeing on the screen was the transcript of a lengthy online messaging session.

"Kyle," she said, moving closer, "you know how I feel about texting when you're supposed to be—*what is* that?"

There, on the screen, was a message from one of Kyle's friends—a kid he had gotten to know at the Christian school he attended: *"I'm going to get to my science project after I download some porn."*

"He's going to download *porn*?" Sharon had to read the message twice to be sure she was seeing it right.

"Come on, Mom," Kyle said. "Don't freak out. It's not that big of a deal—almost all the guys do it."

"Listen to me, Kyle," Sharon said, forgetting all about dinner. "Ever since you were a baby, I've prayed that you will be caught if you're doing anything wrong."

Kyle knew that was true—and usually, according to his calculations, he wound up getting nabbed within about twenty-four hours of any mischief-making.

"And my goal," Sharon continued, "is to keep you pure. Right now, nothing is more important to me than that. When you get married, or even when you're in a dating relationship, you don't want to be carrying around all these destructive images in your mind."

"I think you're overreacting," Kyle said.

Sharon didn't see it that way. And she knew that, deep down, Kyle recognized that pornography was wrong—but that the influence of his peers could easily crowd out anything she or her husband tried to teach him. If she couldn't count on Kyle to look away from the computer screen or refuse to log on to some of the sites his friends recommended, she realized she would have to stand guard on his behalf.

Sharon googled "parental control programs." The search yielded a "Top 10" list, and she chose one that looked like it would work for what she needed. Next, she created a "whitelist" of sites Kyle could visit, as well as a "blacklist" of those he would be denied access to. She began compiling a notebook of passwords and codes so she'd have ready access to any site Kyle visited or any program he ran. Finally, she purchased a program that provided a record of every single keystroke and every screen that popped up—and how long it stayed on the monitor.

"You're invading my privacy!" Kyle protested.

"I'm protecting your purity," Sharon replied.

PRAYER PRINCIPLE

When you monitor your teen's internet use, you are not invading their privacy; you are protecting their purity—and their future.

The more Sharon learned, the more vigilant she became. "It was kind of embarrassing," she laughs, thinking back to the long days of summer when Kyle would ask to hang out at a friend's house. "I would call up these moms I hardly knew and ask what sort of protection they had on their home computer or what search engines or filters their kids had on their phones. Some of them had no idea what I was talking about!"

Even so, Sharon realized that her best efforts could not protect her son. She couldn't be the POS ("Parent over Shoulder") all the time, and with pornography accounting for 30 percent of all internet traffic, her teens were bound to encounter it. Not only that, but even peer-to-peer communication via texting and social media could open the door to a host of unwanted images and messages.

What could she do? What can any of us do?

Poised for Prayer

Those are the type of questions Andy Crouch tackles in his book. The answer to the dark side of technology, he says, isn't just to install internet filters and set limits on things like screen time and social media use. The answer is to value things like character, wisdom, and strong relationships with family and friends over the instant gratification, escapism, and easy entertainment that technology offers. "We are meant," Crouch writes, "not just for thin, virtual connections but for visceral, real connections to one another in this fleeting, temporary, and infinitely beautiful and worthwhile life."[7]

PRAYER PRINCIPLE

Protecting our kids against the dangers of technology involves more than keeping bad stuff out; it involves building good stuff into their lives.

Reading about Andy Crouch's proactive approach to technology use reminded me of Nehemiah, the Old Testament guy who faced threats as real as the ones that stream into our homes via social media and the internet every day. As Nehemiah and his fellow Jews worked to rebuild the walls of Jerusalem, their enemies kept up a constant barrage of insults and attacks. In response, Nehemiah did three things: he posted a guard, made a plan to fight back, and prayed.[8]

We can do these same things today.

We can post a guard. Our kids may think we are the strictest parents in the world (and we need to be prepared for the fact that we won't be very popular in their eyes sometimes), but we need to establish boundaries regarding technology use. In addition to things like installing filters and having access to the passwords on our teens' devices, we need to be intentional about teaching our kids to guard their time, and their hearts, against the mindless scrolling and empty entertainment that screens can deliver—along with feelings of inferiority, loneliness, and depression.

We can make a plan. What this looks like in practice will vary among families, but a key ingredient in any successful strategy is for parents to model the behaviors they want teens to adopt. In the Crouch family, for example, they've adopted ten "commitments" that are observed by both parents and teens—policies designed to put technology in what Andy calls "its proper place." Among these are a commitment to the rhythm of work and rest (intentionally turning devices off for hours, days, and even a whole week during each year); respecting sleep (the Crouches "wake up" before their devices do, and put them "to bed" before they go to sleep); sharing passwords between spouses and granting parents full access to their kids' devices; and designating car time as conversation time rather than having everyone ensconced in their own virtual world.[9]

We can pray. Nehemiah's battle strategy called for unity among the Israelites and a willingness to fight together to keep the whole group safe. Nobody in his company was allowed to work alone; they used a buddy system—with each worker carrying a weapon along with their tools and building materials. At the first sign of an invasion, Nehemiah would have his own buddy sound the trumpet, and the Israelites would close ranks to repel the attackers.

That's how we need to do it. Instead of fighting the internet invasion on our own, let's partner with other parents and with our churches to pray—using our own "sword," which is God's Word, to give life to our prayers.[10] "Where there is real agreement," writes R. A. Torrey, "where the Spirit lays the same burden on two hearts, in all such prayer there is absolutely irresistible power."[11]

Let's ask God to equip our teens with the wisdom to use technology wisely, valuing in-person interactions over virtual connections—things like text messages and snapchats—where there is little to no emotional investment or accountability. Let's pray that our kids will be surrounded by a hedge of protection—a God-ordained filter—as they use their devices and share online content with their peers. And rather than giving into fear or uncertainty as we regard the ever-changing landscape of technology, let's follow Nehemiah's example. "Don't be afraid," he exhorted his people. "Remember the Lord, who is great and awesome, and fight for your families, your sons and your daughters, your wives and your homes."[12]

Prayers You Can Use

Heavenly Father . . .

Whatever is true, whatever is noble, whatever is right, whatever is pure, whatever is admirable—if anything is excellent or praiseworthy—may _____ think about such things.

Philippians 4:8

Set a hedge of protection around _____, one that evil cannot penetrate.

Job 1:10

Let no unwholesome words or pictures have a place on _____'s phone or computer screen. Instead, let all online communication be helpful for building people up according to their needs, so that they may benefit from technology use.

Ephesians 4:29

Prompt _____ to guard what they see, since the eye is the lamp of the body and if the eyes are healthy, the whole body is full of light.

Matthew 6:22–23

When _____ feels lonely or distressed by social media or online content, come to their rescue. May integrity and uprightness protect _____ as they put their hope in you.

Psalm 25:16–21

Don't let _____ look with approval on anything that is vile. May they have no part in what faithless or perverse people do, and have nothing to do with evil or any kind of slander—whether it is done face-to-face, over the telephone, or online.

Psalm 101:3–4

May _____ grow up healthy in God, robust in love, and refusing to go along with the empty-headed, mindless crowd who have lost touch not just with God but with reality itself.

Ephesians 4:16–18 MSG

Guard _____'s heart and mind so that they will not spend time gossiping or saying things they shouldn't, whether online or in person.

1 Timothy 5:13

Let _____ have nothing to do with the fruitless deeds of darkness, since it is shameful to even mention what the disobedient do in secret. If _____ is involved in anything dark or evil, expose it with the light of your love.

Ephesians 5:11–13

Search _____ and know their heart. Point out anything that offends you and lead them along the path of everlasting life.

Psalm 139:23–24

You see all that _____ does—every website they visit, every image they post, every online path they take. Don't let them be ensnared by the evil deeds of the wicked or be led astray by their own great folly.

Proverbs 5:21–23

Cause _____ to walk in the way of love when they go online, rejecting anything that bears even a hint of sexual immorality or of any kind of impurity, greed, obscenity, foolish talk, or coarse joking.

Ephesians 5:3–4

Help _____ to be alert and sober-minded regarding the dangers that can come via the internet. Protect _____ so that they will not be devoured by the enemy.

1 Peter 5:8

Open my eyes and teach me, Lord, so I will be equipped to set limits and establish rules for internet use in our house. Give me wisdom, and cause my teens to listen to my instruction and not forsake my teaching in this important area.

Proverbs 1:8

Chapter 17

Praying for Protection from Drinking

Wine is a mocker and beer a brawler;
whoever is led astray by them is not wise.
Proverbs 20:1

I went to college at the University of Virginia. At the time, the school had an abysmal football program, a top academic rating, and a reputation for throwing some of the nation's best (or worst, depending on your perspective) cocktail parties. The local grocery store—part of a national chain—welcomed students back to school every year by stacking cases of beer into towering pyramids, and it prided itself on selling more of the stuff than any other store in the country.

I lived with a couple of brainiacs named Susan and Barbie. Susan, I discovered, had been an SAT whiz kid with a vocabulary the size of Texas, and in an effort to upgrade our verbal repertoire as we discussed the university's party scene, she began posting useful words on the walls of our apartment. *Obstreperous*, I learned, could be employed to describe behavior that was marked by unruly or aggressive noisiness. *Temerarious* signaled a tendency to be rash, reckless, or daring. And *corybantic*—which quickly became a household favorite, in light of some of the fraternity dances we attended—meant "wild" and "frenzied."

In addition to being incredibly smart, Susan and Barbie were deeply committed Christians. When we realized how much attention our "vocabulary in the foyer" program garnered among our friends, we branched out into Scripture memory, taping index cards to the walls of our kitchen. One card that never failed to draw comments was Proverbs 23:29–35:

> Who has woe? Who has sorrow?
>> Who has strife? Who has complaints?
>> Who has needless bruises? Who has bloodshot eyes?
> Those who linger over wine,
>> who go to sample bowls of mixed wine.
> Do not gaze at wine when it is red,
>> when it sparkles in the cup,
>> when it goes down smoothly!
> In the end it bites like a snake
>> and poisons like a viper.
> Your eyes will see strange sights,
>> and your mind imagine confusing things.
> You will be like one sleeping on the high seas,
>> lying on top of the rigging.
> "They hit me," you will say, "but I'm not hurt!
>> They beat me, but I don't feel it!
> When will I wake up
>> so I can find another drink?"

"*That's* not in the Bible!" a visitor would protest.

"Oh, yes it is!" we'd crow, opening our Bibles to prove ourselves right—and cementing our status as total nerds.

Back then, we laughed at the drunks—and marveled when they managed to show up for class the next day. Once I had teens of my own, though, I stopped laughing. There is nothing funny about underage drinking, and the fact that so many parents facilitate it ("*Somebody* has to teach these kids to drink responsibly before they go off to college!") only makes the situation more complicated. I thought things might improve after a group of high school athletes in our town were caught drinking and had to forfeit their season, but I was wrong. "Did the kids learn a lesson?" I asked one parent. "Oh, yes," she answered. "They learned to not have their picture taken with a beer in their hand."

I wish I could say teen alcohol use is a public school problem or a private school problem or a problem in households where parents drink—or where they don't. The truth, as one of my teacher-friends lamented the other day, is that alcohol is *everywhere* . . .

◦◦ ◦◦ ◦◦

Marla eyed the carnage in her daughter's bedroom. The homecoming dance was being held that night, and her daughter, Isabelle, had invited a group of her girlfriends over to get ready for the party. It had been fun to listen to them help each other with their hair and makeup, and from the amount of clothing strewn all over the floor, Marla figured the girls must have tried on several outfits apiece. Reaching down to tidy one of the piles, Marla's hand brushed against a bottle. The label said Gatorade . . . but the liquid left in the bottle was clear.

Marla removed the cap and sniffed. Not Gatorade. Vodka. Marla sighed.

Just last month, Isabelle had hosted a larger party, one where several teens had brought alcohol. Marla and her husband had confiscated the bottles and shut things down, a move that left Isabelle in tears. "How could you embarrass me like that in front of my friends?" she exclaimed.

"Embarrass *you*?" Marla countered. "How could you put us in such an awkward position? We *like* your friends—and we never want to kick kids out of our house."

"But I didn't *know* people would bring anything," Isabelle wailed. "The kids all know that you and Dad are not big partyers and that you don't let kids drink. They know this is a Christian house; how was I supposed to know they would bring beer and stuff?"

Marla had wanted to believe Isabelle—that she really hadn't known what her friends would do—but her instincts said otherwise. Isabelle's tone when she talked about their house being "Christian" sounded more mocking than sad, and Marla suspected that her daughter's disappointment over the way the party had ended was not that her friends had brought alcohol, but that they had been caught. Now, holding the repurposed Gatorade bottle and thinking back to the laughter she'd overheard while the girls were getting dressed, Marla realized what every parenting expert (and, indeed, every parent) knows: friends, rather than family, are the primary influence in a teen's life.

PRAYER PRINCIPLE

Peers are the primary influence in a young person's life. Ask God to choose your teen's companions.

Isabelle, Marla decided, knew exactly what her friends were up to—and she clearly wanted to please them more than she wanted to please her parents. Or God.

God.

Marla wondered what *he* thought of Isabelle's behavior. Isabelle was well known as a leader in her church's youth group and, in fact, she had plans to work at a Christian camp that summer. Her behavior certainly wasn't lining up with her beliefs, and Marla figured she and her husband could not, in good conscience, let her go to the camp. At least not without letting her bosses know they might have a drinker—and a liar—on their hands.

"It's okay," the camp director said, when Marla's husband outlined the problem. "We get teens all the time who are torn between serving God and pleasing their peers. Let Isabelle come work with us; she'll be surrounded by other Christians, and that—more than anything you could say or do—could prompt her to make a real decision to follow Christ."

Marla felt relieved. If nothing else, Isabelle would be gone for six weeks, safely tucked away doing laundry or cleaning cabins at a camp where there was not apt to be access to alcohol. Six whole weeks when Marla wouldn't have to worry about who her daughter was with or what she was doing.

There was only one problem.

Isabelle did not want to go.

After the homecoming dance, Marla told Isabelle she knew she had been drinking and that she was grounded for a month. "You're lucky, though," she said. "The camp still wants you to work there this summer."

"Well, I don't want to work there anymore," Isabelle said. "I'm not going. And you can't make me."

Marla knew her daughter was right. She and her husband could not *make* Isabelle go to the camp—and even if they could, they knew better than to send a sullen, uncooperative teen to a place where her attitude could poison countless younger teens.

Not knowing what else to do, Marla prayed.

> Take away Isabelle's hard heart of stone and replace it with one of flesh. Give her a heart to know you as Lord; may she return to you with all her heart. May she put aside the deeds of darkness and put on the armor of light.[1]

Every time Marla opened her Bible, she found another promise from God—something that seemed to speak directly to her concerns. Sometimes the prompt seemed like it had been tailormade for her daughter, like when Elijah went up against all the prophets of Baal and issued a challenge to the Israelites: "How long will you waver between two opinions?" the prophet said. "If the LORD is God, follow him; but if Baal is God, follow him."[2]

"Don't let Isabelle waver between following the world and following you," she prayed. "Let her decide to follow you with her whole heart."

Things got worse before they got better.

First, Isabelle got a speeding ticket. Then she was rear-ended on her way to school. And then, just a week after the first accident, she wrecked a second car. Thankfully no one was hurt, but Marla could not imagine what God was doing. Had he forgotten her prayers?

And then one day, a week or so after the second car wreck, Isabelle made an announcement over dinner. "I'm going to work at that camp," she said.

Marla and her husband exchanged a look. *What was Isabelle cooking up now?*

"I figure," she continued with a smile, "that God is trying to get my attention with all of these bad things that keep happening, and that I need to listen to him before I get killed or something."

Marla hid her own smile. *God*, she thought, *certainly did work in mysterious ways.*

And a few months later, when Isabelle returned from the camp, it was obvious that God had continued to work. Isabelle had painted a sign that she hung over the desk in her bedroom. On it were just three words: *TWO FEET IN.*

"What does that mean?" Marla asked.

"It means I'm sick of wavering," Isabelle said. "I'm sick of living with one foot in the world and one foot in my faith. I decided I need to put both feet in and follow God."

Poised for Prayer

When Marla told me her story, I wondered how she had stayed so calm during the long months when Isabelle was following hard after the drinking crowd. When I had my own run-ins with teens and alcohol, I had felt angry. Confused. Betrayed, even. I didn't understand how my kids could profess Christ with their mouths and then turn around and make choices that dishonored my husband and me and ran so contrary to God's commands.

"Oh, I definitely got mad," Marla said. "And my own heart grew hard—maybe as a defense against the fear I was feeling. I didn't like the woman I thought Isabelle was becoming.

"And," she continued, "the fact that she was nursing a hangover the morning she left for that camp didn't make things any easier. I knew God could work in her and through her to accomplish his best purposes in her life, but I had no idea how he would do it. I was just glad to get her out of the house."

So what happened? What changed Isabelle's heart, making her want to live "two feet in"?

"I think the camp director was right," Marla acknowledged. "Peers are so much more influential than parents—for bad, and for good. And when Isabelle found herself surrounded by kids who truly loved Jesus—the real Jesus, not some watered-down version that couldn't captivate a teen's attention—that rubbed off. And it stuck.

"I also think," she continued, "that Isabelle knew we loved her. Deep down, she knew that what she was doing was wrong, but we couldn't change her behavior. All we could do was keep the door open and pray as we waited for God to work in her heart.

"And," she added, "it's not like Isabelle turned into some perfect person overnight. She's still learning what it looks like to follow God with both feet. But she's making progress. She's paying attention to God's commands, and—like it says in Isaiah 48:18—she knows what it feels like to experience his peace."

Listening to Marla talk, I couldn't help but think about the parable of the prodigal son, the fellow who squandered his entire inheritance in wild living before, dirt-poor and starving, he came to his senses, acknowledged his sin, and returned, broken, to his father's household.[3] As Jesus tells the story, the father saw his son when he was still a long way off. Dropping everything, he gathered up his robes and ran—ran!—to meet his boy, throwing his arms open wide to welcome his wayward son home.

That father's heart must have hurt, just like ours often does. He might have even gotten angry sometimes. But I am convinced that this dad never stopped loving his son or looking expectantly for his return. As parents, we need to be equally faithful in love—and equally expectant in prayer—as we wait for God to move.

We can't change our kids, but he can.

PRAYER PRINCIPLE

We must be faithful in love and expectant in prayer
as we wait for God to work in our teen's life.

Let's ask God to surround our kids with people who will exert positive peer pressure in their lives, people who will point them toward the "real" Jesus in whom they can find complete and genuine joy (versus the counterfeit kind that the party culture offers).[4] And when we catch our kids doing something wrong—whether they break a curfew, squander their money, or show up for work at a Christian camp with a hangover—let's remember that God's ultimate goal is not to punish but to restore, and that the world's power to ruin their lives is nothing compared to God's ability to redeem them.

Yes, our teens need to face the consequences of their behavior (and we need to be quick to seek professional help if we suspect their drinking is becoming a recurrent or serious problem), but let's parent with grace. Let's embrace our kids in such a way that they know that, no matter what happened, we still love them.

Just like our heavenly Father still loves wayward, mistake-making us.

Prayers You Can Use

Heavenly Father . . .

Let _____ thirst for a drink from your river of delights rather than for anything that alcohol offers, for with you is the fountain of life.   *Psalm 36:8–9*

Teach _____ what is best; direct them in the way they should go. Cause _____ to pay attention to your commands so that they will experience peace like a river and well-being like the waves of the sea.   *Isaiah 48:17–18*

Cause _____ to live a decent life for all to see, not participating in the darkness of wild parties and drunkenness but being clothed with the presence of Christ.   *Romans 13:13–14 NLT*

Don't let _____ be drunk with alcohol, because that will ruin their life. Instead, fill _____ with the Holy Spirit.

Ephesians 5:18 NLT

Show _____ that they will become a slave to whatever they choose to obey—peers, a craving for alcohol, a desire for popularity, or any other sin. Prompt them to obey you and enjoy righteous living.   *Romans 6:16*

Help _____ to live by the Spirit so that they will not want to gratify the desires of the sinful nature. Instead of being filled with debauchery or drunkenness, may _____ be filled with the fruit of the Spirit and live a life marked by love, joy, peace, forbearance, kindness, goodness, faithfulness, gentleness, and self-control.   *Galatians 5:19–23*

Don't let _____ waver between two opinions; prompt _____ to serve you, not peers or alcohol.

1 Kings 18:21

Give _____ an eagerness to do your will, turning away from things like debauchery, lust, drunkenness, carousing, and reckless, wild living—even when their friends act surprised by their good behavior and heap abuse on them.

1 Peter 4:2–4

When the enemy tries to use things like alcohol or peer pressure to cause _____ to stumble, give them an alert and sober mind to stand firm and resist Satan's evil schemes. Remind them that they stand with godly teens all over the world who face similar temptations, persecution from peers, and suffering.

1 Peter 5:8–10

Cause _____ to listen to your commands and become wise instead of joining with those who drink too much alcohol or gorge themselves on meat, for drunkards and gluttons become poor, and drowsiness clothes them in rags.

Proverbs 23:19–21

Do not let _____ be tempted beyond what they can bear, but provide a way out so that they can endure it.

1 Corinthians 10:13

When sinful people entice _____, saying "Come along with us," give them the strength and courage to stay far away from their paths.

Proverbs 1:10–15

Teach _____ to say no to ungodliness and worldly passions and to live an upright and godly life among their peers.

Titus 2:11–12

Prompt _____ to live a life of moral excellence, which leads to knowing you better, which leads to self-control—so that ultimately they will be productive and useful.

2 Peter 1:5–8

When I need to discipline _____, don't let them resent it. Remind _____ that you discipline those you love, and that my correction is a sign of my love.

Proverbs 3:11–12

Chapter 18

Praying for Sexual Purity

*Do you not know that your bodies are temples of the
Holy Spirit, who is in you, whom you have received
from God? You are not your own; you were bought
at a price. Therefore honor God with your bodies.*

1 Corinthians 6:19–20

"What's your idea of a perfect week?"

My friend Jim led a Bible study for a group of middle school
guys. As usual, he opened the discussion with an icebreaker question, something lighthearted to help the group get to know one
another and jump-start the discussion. He figured their answers
would be some combination of sports victories, homework passes,
or—since they lived in the shadow of the Colorado Rockies—
ideal conditions for snowboarding. Instead, one of the thirteen-
year-olds quickly weighed in with this:

"My perfect week? That would be one where I got a sex text
every day for seven days straight!"

The other kids laughed and agreed—yes, that would be
amazing.

Jim was stunned—these were Christian kids, leaders in the
church youth group. Sexting? Really?

When Jim told me his story, I was less surprised. I'd seen the teen magazine headlines in the grocery store checkout line ("7 Tips for Sending Your Best Sexts Ever!"), and I'd recently talked with a group of high school girls about sex and dating. Our discussion covered what they believed to be true about things like *appearance* ("the more attractive you are, the better you are"), *reputation* ("nobody will judge you, or think less of you, if you mess around"), *self-image* ("the faster you are, the more guys will like you and the more you will like yourself"), and *sex* ("it's okay as long as you love the person"). We'd also talked about what they called the trade-off: guys will exchange emotional intimacy (saying "I love you") to get sex, while girls will give physical intimacy in order to receive feelings of love.

My daughter Hillary was part of that conversation. She didn't say much, and I worried that she might be sitting there hating life, wishing she could be anyplace other than in a room full of mostly older girls listening to her mom talk about sex. She told me afterward that she had, in fact, wondered about how the evening would go—but her fears (and mine) were allayed by the group's very positive response; one girl actually said that Hillary was "lucky" that her mother could talk about "this stuff."

Truth be told, I *didn't* talk to Hillary—or any of my kids—all that much when it came to squirmy subjects like sex. As a youth group leader, I found it far easier to give a "sex talk" to a group of fifty middle schoolers than to have a heart-to-heart with one of my own teens about what they ought to be doing—or not doing—with their bodies. And in an age when entire churches can split over questions about things like homosexuality and gender identity, it can be hard for parents to know how to discuss biblical truth without sounding judgmental. As one of my friends said when her son told her he was gay, "He doesn't want me to love him 'anyway'; he wants me to love him, period. I do—but he doesn't see it that way."

If parents are uncomfortable talking about sex, it's a safe bet we aren't doing a whole lot of proactive praying about it either. If you picked up this book and flipped straight to this chapter, my guess is that you suspect—or know—that your teen has already gone farther down the road than you would like, and you're looking for a way to pray them out of a bad situation. (That's okay, by the way. The Bible is full of "rescue me!" prayers—and frankly, the darker things look, the brighter God shines.)

Maybe, like many Christian parents, you thought your teen's relationship with Christ would offer a measure of purity protection. Maybe you were counting on your church's youth group leader to convince your son to set some sexual boundaries—and honor them. Maybe you hoped your daughter was safe because she hangs out with such a "nice" crowd.

Or maybe, like the mom in this story, you simply thought "it" could never happen in your family . . .

∾ ∾ ∾

"Ninety percent of families have trouble with their teens, and they don't even know about it."

Clare turned to her friend Nancy, who sat in the passenger seat as the two women made their way toward a prayer leaders retreat sponsored by Moms in Prayer. "Did you hear that?" she asked.

Nancy nodded. The two had been listening to a Christian radio broadcast during the drive, and they were getting an earful of parenting advice.

"Ninety percent!" Clare repeated. "I feel *so* sorry for those people."

Clare drove on, but her thoughts were far from the highway. She knew her fourteen-year-old son, Troy, could be mischievous, but as she listened to the harrowing tales of other people's teens, she counted her blessings. Troy was an only child who attended a Christian school, and Clare thought she pretty much knew what was going on in his life. Thinking about all those unfortunate parents—that poor 90 percent!—she was glad she didn't have to worry about *her* son.

At the retreat, Clare found herself soaking up biblical teaching on all manner of subjects, including a breakout session on how to pray for your teen's sexual purity. When the speaker offered a five-page prayer handout on the subject, Clare took a copy. It looked like a valuable tool—and who knew? Maybe one of the moms in her prayer group back home would need it.

Clare also found herself paired with a woman named Cindy, a mother whose two sons were about the same age as Troy. On their last day together, Cindy prayed for Clare, using the words of Isaiah 58:11 (NASB): "Father God," she prayed, "guide Clare and satisfy her desire in scorched places. Give strength to her bones. Let her be like a watered garden, like a spring whose waters do not fail."

Clare nodded her assent, agreeing with Cindy's words. But her prayer partner wasn't finished. "Lord, give strength to Clare's *tired* and *weary* bones. Give her *perseverance* during times of scorching."

As Cindy continued to pray, zeroing in on Clare's apparent weariness and her need for strength, Clare found herself pulling back. *Hold on a minute!* she thought to herself. *I only have one son—and he's a pretty good boy. I mean, thanks for the prayers and all—but honestly, my life is just not that hard!*

Still wondering what Cindy could have meant with all of her "scorching" prayers, Clare pulled into her driveway after the retreat. She was on top of the world—spiritually renewed and ready to pray for her family with a fresh enthusiasm. Troy came out to help carry her bags, but was uncharacteristically silent. "What's up?" Clare asked.

"Nothing," Troy mumbled.

"Nothing" turned out to be something that left Clare reeling. While she was gone, Troy had been caught masturbating in a thicket near their home, along with a neighbor—a younger boy—from his school. Like many praying parents, Clare had often asked God to let her son get caught if he was plotting, or doing, anything wrong—but never in her wildest dreams could she have imagined something like this. It had to be some sort of a sick mistake.

"Boys will be boys," Clare's husband said when she asked him about what had happened. She knew Bill was upset, and that he was just trying to comfort her, but his words rang hollow—particularly given the five-page handout on sexual purity that now seemed to be burning a hole in her purse. All of those verses about honoring God with our bodies did not add up to anything that could endorse the picture of two boys masturbating together in the bushes!

Clare was crushed. She felt uncertain and alone, and she wondered where she had gone wrong in raising her son. The other boy's mother, who had caught the boys, blamed Troy for what had happened. She didn't want to discuss the matter, let alone forgive anyone—and Clare found herself wondering whether she would be able to forgive Troy either. Suddenly she knew why Cindy, her retreat prayer partner, felt led to pray all that stuff about needing strength.

In the days that followed, it seemed that Clare's only comfort came from the Lord. His gentle whisper pierced her heart: "Haven't *I* forgiven *you*?" A lifetime of stupid mistakes flooded Clare's mind, and she realized that what Troy needed more than anything else was unconditional love. He *knew* what he had done was wrong; the important thing now was to get him back on the right track. Shame, Clare knew, could be a deadly evil. Thankful that the lines of communication were open, she and Bill began to pray for Troy's healing, and that he would find acceptance from them—and, more importantly, from God.

Over time, several factors contributed to Troy's spiritual and emotional restoration. "God is so creative in the way he has worked in Troy's life," Clare told me. "For example, our city hosted a Pure Excitement rally.[1] Troy heard Joe White—author of a book called *Pure Excitement*—speak, and now all he can talk about is waiting until he gets married before he even kisses a girl."

"Ultimately," Clare went on, "the things that Satan planned for Troy's ruin and defeat are the things that God used for his good. Our neighbors still won't talk to us—but even that is something God is using to build Troy's character and to teach us about forgiveness. We are still working our way through everything, but God has graciously allowed us to see how powerfully he can work, and that his heart is to redeem even the worst situation."

PRAYER PRINCIPLE

God's heart is to redeem, and his power
often shines brightest in the darkness.

Poised for Prayer

Like many Christian parents, I have a hefty collection of parenting books, and when it comes to sexual purity, all the "experts" agree—it's best to talk about sex and dating *before* our kids start to date. We should, they say, teach our kids to avoid sexual immorality by learning to control their bodies and not taking advantage of someone else, and by recognizing that their bodies are not their own, but God's, and that they are the place where his Spirit dwells.[2] These parallel concepts—self-control and honor for God and for others—can help our teens set limits on physical intimacy and envision what it looks like, in a dating relationship, to live out verses like Philippians 2:3–4, doing nothing out of selfishness but looking to the interests of others.

But what about kids who have already crossed those lines? What if you're reading this chapter, knowing that your son or daughter has, as Solomon put it, "aroused or awakened" love or desire prematurely?[3] What if your teen is experimenting with homosexuality, pornography, or any other sexual practice that runs counter to God's design? What then?

I love what Clare said about her son Troy—that he knew what he was doing was wrong, and that shame, left unchecked in his life, could be a deadly evil.

In the Garden of Eden, in their pre-fall existence, Adam and Eve were "both naked, and they felt no shame."[4] Shame entered the world when sin did, and it has been working to disconnect us from God ever since. We know our flaws—our teens know *their* flaws—and that sense of unworthiness can move us, lightning-quick, from conviction (which is good) to condemnation (which isn't). How easy it is for us, and for our teens, to regard our mistakes and think, *How could God possibly love us, with all that we've done?*

PRAYER PRINCIPLE

Shame can be the single biggest hindrance
to our teen's connection with Christ.

Here's the thing, though: God knew we would mess up—and that our kids would too. But convicting them of sin—and making them want to repent—is not up to us. That's the Holy Spirit's job.[5] Our job, Scripture says, is restoration: "If another believer is overcome by some sin, you who are godly should gently and humbly help that person back onto the right path."[6]

When our teens are ensnared in sexual sin, we should certainly ask the Holy Spirit to convict them, to "open their eyes and turn them from darkness to light, and from the power of Satan to God."[7] At the same time, though, we need to reassure them of God's love—and of ours. Satan would love to drive a wedge between you and your teen. And he'd love to separate your teen from God, making them feel worthless and ashamed.

The truth is, though, that nothing—*nothing!*—can separate our kids from God's love.[8]

Let's pray that our teens will come before God the way the nameless woman did when she was caught in adultery. They may stand accused—by Satan, by their peers, and by their own hearts—but let's ask God to help our kids have eyes only for Jesus. Let's ask him to open their ears so they can hear him speak these life-giving words:

"Neither do I condemn you. Go now and leave your life of sin."[9]

Prayers You Can Use

Heavenly Father . . .

When _____ experiences conviction of sin, remind them that you are the God who brings the dead back to life and who creates new things—including reputations and purity—out of nothing.

Romans 4:17 NLT

Equip _____ to be self-controlled and live in holiness and honor—not in passionate lust, like the example so often set by people who do not know you.   *1 Thessalonians 4:4–5*

Do not let any part of _____'s body become an instrument of evil to serve sin. Instead, may _____ use their whole body as an instrument to do what is right for the glory of God.

Romans 6:12–13 NLT

Teach _____ to take every thought captive and make it obedient to Christ.   *2 Corinthians 10:5*

Create in _____ a clean heart, and renew a loyal spirit within them. Give _____ joy and a spirit that is willing to obey you.

Psalm 51:10–12 NLT

When _____ is on a date, remind them not to do anything out of selfishness or vanity, but to be humble, valuing their date above themselves and treating them the way they would want someone to treat their future spouse.   *Philippians 2:3*

Guard _____'s heart in romantic relationships, for that determines the course of their life. *Proverbs 4:23 NLT*

Prompt _____ to flee from sexual immorality, since sexual sin is against one's own body, and our bodies are the temple of the Holy Spirit. *1 Corinthians 6:18-19*

When _____ thinks they are standing strong, remind them to be careful not to fall! When _____ is tempted, provide a way out. *1 Corinthians 10:12-13*

When _____ is caught in sexual sin, remind them that your mercies begin afresh each morning. Put people in their life who will restore them gently.

Lamentations 3:23 NLT; Galatians 6:1

Surround _____ with people who will teach them to be temperate, worthy of respect, self-controlled, sound in faith, loving, patient, and pure. *Titus 2:2-5*

Keep _____'s heart from growing hard and being drawn away from you so they indulge in every kind of impurity. Keep _____'s heart soft and sensitive to your Holy Spirit.

Ephesians 4:18-19

Put to death all things in _____'s life that belong to their earthly nature: sexual immorality, impurity, lust, evil desires, and greed, which is idolatry. *Colossians 3:5*

Keep _____'s heart from being drawn to evil; protect them from snares and traps set by evildoers. *Psalm 141:4, 9*

Give _____ the grace to believe there is no condemnation for those who are in Christ Jesus, and that nothing can separate them from your love. *Romans 8:1, 39*

Chapter 19

Praying for Protection from Drugs

Don't you realize that you become the slave of whatever you choose to obey? You can be a slave to sin, which leads to death, or you can choose to obey God, which leads to righteous living.

Romans 6:16 NLT

"Why would you do drugs?"

Ask that question to any random group of teens—47 percent of whom admit to having used an illegal drug by the time they graduate from high school[1]—and you're apt to get any number of answers.

It makes me feel good. Drugs interact with the neurochemistry of the brain to produce feelings of pleasure, a temporary euphoria ("getting high") that can make a teen feel better, whether they're alone or with friends.

It's an escape. Depression, anxiety, stress-related disorders, and physical pain can make teens want to self-medicate, using drugs as a way to minimize symptoms or numb physical and emotional hurts.

It will help me do better. Many teens feel intense pressure to perform—academically or athletically—and they see illegal and prescription drugs as a way to enhance their abilities and meet expectations of teachers, parents, and coaches.

I just wanted to try it. Adolescents are naturally curious and eager to seek new experiences—particularly those that seem daring or even dangerous—and many teens experiment with drugs simply to see what it feels like.

I want to fit in. By far the most common reason kids do drugs is because their peers are—or they *think* they are. The desire for acceptance and belonging is a powerful motivator. And not just among teens. Consider the first-century believers who had seen Jesus do incredible miracles but kept silent about their faith for fear that they'd be put out of the synagogue. "They loved human praise," Scripture says, "more than praise from God."[2]

All of these reasons—and plenty of others, including a family history of substance abuse or other childhood trauma—can make a teen want to smoke pot or even experiment with "harder" drugs like heroin or cocaine. But the fastest-growing drug problem in our country (and the one that impacts teens the most) isn't any of these things. It's prescription drugs.

And as my friend Janie will tell you, no amount of parental desire to rescue a child from that pit is enough . . .

෨ ෨ ෨

"He's going to die."

Janie gripped her husband's hand—the one she had silently clung to during the night when she couldn't form words into prayers—and gave voice to her deepest fear. Their son Isaac was slipping away. The nightmare was starting again.

Janie replayed Isaac's teen years in her mind. Was there a signal she had missed? Something she and her husband Charlie should have picked up on? Something they could have done?

She didn't think so.

Isaac, the youngest of five brothers, had always had a wild streak—one that other kids found appealing. Never one to be left behind, he did everything his big brothers did, whether it meant jumping into a pool when he couldn't swim or hopping onto a bike with no training wheels and pedaling like mad. A gifted musician, Isaac loved playing in the praise band at church (a job that, as he saw it, was much more fun than his earlier role as an acolyte), and everywhere he went, Isaac made friends. He made people feel loved, Janie thought, whether they were in the cool crowd at school or the kid from the youth group nobody else wanted to sit with.

Isaac checked all the boxes. Sure, Janie had gotten her share of late-night phone calls—car wrecks, curfew violations, even some run-ins with alcohol—but what mother of five teen boys hadn't been there? Janie was quick to ask her Bible study friends to keep Isaac in their prayers—she knew he was always pushing the limits—but for the most part, she wasn't overly worried.

Until she got a call that was worse than the rest.

Isaac was on the way to the hospital. He had been out late—too late—watching basketball with his older brothers. When they left the restaurant where they'd been eating (and, Janie knew, drinking), a stranger had rushed out of the shadows and, without warning, smashed Isaac across the face with an iron pipe. The fact that it was a case of mistaken identity didn't change the reality that Isaac would be in surgery—and on medication—for a long, long time.

Which led to an addiction to prescription painkillers.

Which led to an addiction to illegal drugs when the prescription ran out.

Which led to a long stint in rehab.

Several rehab programs actually. Janie watched her son's three-year journey—two steps forward, one step back—and filled her prayer journal with Scripture. "You were dead because of your sins," she wrote. "Then God made you alive with Christ, for he forgave all our sins. He canceled the record of the charges against us and took it away by nailing it to the cross."[3]

Janie knew that God did not condemn her son, and neither did she. Isaac had lost a lot—his college chances, his job, his girlfriend—but he was alive. And he seemed to be making progress. And when he hit the one-year-sober mark—365 days of being drug and alcohol free—they had all celebrated.

Now, though, things were spiraling out of control.

Charlie had taken Isaac to get his wisdom teeth out. He explained to the oral surgeon that he could not, under any circumstances, administer pain medication that contained fentanyl, a highly addictive substance that could activate Isaac's craving.

The doctor ignored the warning, and within weeks, Isaac was looking for drugs—opioids, painkillers, heroin—anywhere he could get them. He left home. Janie was sure that, this time, her son would die.

"Not on my watch," Charlie replied, sounding more confident than he felt.

Charlie found Isaac and checked him into yet another rehab facility—one that included outpatient services so he could do the hard work of recovery while also rebuilding his life. Meanwhile, Janie did the only thing she knew to do: she prayed. And she continued to reach out to her son, letting him know how much he was loved.

"I sent prayers and Scriptures to Isaac," she told me, "especially Jeremiah 29:11. I wanted Isaac to know that God wanted to prosper him, not harm him, and that he had good plans for his life.

"Not only that," she continued, "but I wanted Isaac to know what every addict—and I guess every parent—needs to hear: that God is bigger than his addiction, and that he loves him."

PRAYER PRINCIPLE

God is bigger and more powerful than any addiction.

Well aware that parents tend to isolate themselves when their family is going through a dark time ("There is just so much shame," Janie says), she also reached out to her praying friends.

"I knew I needed people who would pray," she acknowledged, "people who would stand in the gap on our behalf, especially during those weeks and months when it was hard for Charlie and me to find words. I can't imagine going through what we went through without God—or without our community of prayer partners.[4]

"I also knew," she continued, "that my desire to rescue my child—to deliver Isaac, to heal him and make him whole—was not enough. I was helpless. But God wasn't. And it was his desire to heal and deliver my son."

Today, Isaac runs a successful construction company and enjoys life as a newlywed. Like Janie, he is quick to share his redemption story with anyone who asks—and he gets asked often.

"When people know you're willing to talk," Janie says, "they come out of the woodwork. People want to be free from the bondage of addiction. And even though I don't know how everyone's story will end, I know this: our stories belong to God.

"And prayer always releases the power of God for the purpose of God."

Poised for Prayer

Reflecting on Janie's words, I was struck by her desire—and her inability—to rescue her son. Every parent has been there at one point or another, and it can be incredibly painful when we cannot "fix" our kids' problems or protect them from pain.

But that's where our prayers come in.

As Paul told the Corinthian believers, things got so bad at one point in their journey that he and his companions were sure they would die. But they didn't. God rescued them—and they knew he would do it again. "You and your prayers," Paul wrote, "are part of the rescue operation . . . I can see your faces even now, lifted in praise for God's deliverance of us, a rescue in which your prayers played such a crucial part."[5]

God's heart is to deliver our teens. And our prayers are part of the rescue operation.

PRAYER PRINCIPLE

God's heart is to heal and deliver our teens; our prayers are part of the rescue operation.

Yet it can sometimes be hard to know how to pray. Like many parents who believe in the power of praying God's Word, Janie struggled at first to find verses that spoke to her need. The Bible doesn't talk about pot, opioids, cocaine, or other drugs. If we want to pray the Scriptures over an addiction, where do we start?

In Janie's case, a prayer shared by a friend became her daily go-to:

> O blessed Lord, you ministered to all who came to you: Look with compassion upon all who through addiction have lost their health and freedom. Restore to them the assurance of your unfailing mercy; remove from them the fears that beset them; strengthen them in the work of their recovery; and to those who care for them, give patient understanding and persevering love. Amen.[6]

Reading this prayer, I couldn't help but see God's promises undergirding the words:

Jesus came to bind up broken hearts and set captives free. (Isaiah 61:1)

God's mercies never fail; they are new every morning. (Lamentations 3:22–23)

Jesus' peace replaces our fear. (John 14:27)

God strengthens us when we are weak. (Isaiah 40:29)

The Lord always cares for the caregivers, directing our hearts into God's love and Christ's perseverance. (2 Thessalonians 3:5)

Teen drug use is, as Janie said, a form of bondage. It's a way that Satan holds our kids captive in darkness. But they are not the only ones suffering. Parents often find themselves in prison too—a prison of shame and confusion, with bars spun from the steel of Satan's lies: *You have failed as a parent. People will judge you. You and your teen will never be free. God has abandoned you.*

I'm not inventing these words; they reflect comments I've heard over and over again from families who have struggled with addiction.

So as we pray for our teens, let's come alongside one another, being quick to extend love and grace, whether we're the ones struggling or another part of our body is hurting. Let's begin and end our prayers as Romans 8 does, with the twin promises of "no condemnation" and "no separation" from God and his unfailing love.[7]

Prayers You Can Use

Heavenly Father . . .

Don't let _____ be a slave to sin, but give them a permanent place in your family. *John 8:34–35*

Put people in _____'s path who will gently teach them. Cause them to come to their senses so they will believe the truth and escape from the trap of drugs and lies that Satan uses to hold people captive. *2 Timothy 2:25–26*

Do not let _____ be afraid or put to shame. Teach _____ and give them peace. Do not let drugs or any other weapon prevail against them. *Isaiah 54:4–17*

Demolish any strongholds of lying, rebellion, and drug use in _____'s life. Remove anything that gets in the way of their knowledge of you, and cause their thought life to be obedient to Christ. *2 Corinthians 10:5*

Do not let _____ conform to the world's pattern of drug use, but transform and renew their minds so they will approve of your good, pleasing, and perfect will. *Romans 12:2*

Help _____ to see the truth—that people who use drugs and who encourage others to do so are bent on stealing, killing, and destroying. Prompt them to turn to you, knowing that your plan is to give them a rich and satisfying life.

John 10:10 NLT

Remind _____ that their body is your temple. It may look ruined now, but don't let them be afraid. Equip _____ to trust you to fill them with your glory—greater glory than ever before—and grant them peace. *Haggai 1:9; 2:5-9*

Help _____ persevere in trials, relying on your strength instead of on drugs. Equip _____ to stand the test and receive the crown of life you have promised to those who love you.

James 1:12

Prompt _____ to take responsibility when they are tempted, not blaming you but recognizing the strength of their own evil desires. Keep _____ from giving in to those desires, since they lead to sin and death. Protect _____ from deception.

James 1:13-16

Keep _____ safe from the traps that evildoers set, including the snares of illegal drugs and peer pressure.

Psalm 141:9

Open _____'s eyes to see that drugs are a way that may seem right, but in the end they lead to death.

Proverbs 14:12

Come alongside _____ when they are tempted or going through hard times, and then show them how to come alongside other people in their struggles. May _____ experience the full measure of your comfort.

2 Corinthians 1:3–5 MSG

Set _____ free, and help them stand firm. Do not let _____ be burdened by a yoke of slavery to drugs or to any other evil.

Galatians 5:1

Remind _____ that there is no condemnation for anyone who is in Christ Jesus, and that nothing—no addiction, no past mistakes, no powers of hell—can separate them from your love.

Romans 8:1, 38–39

Chapter 20

Praying for Sin to Be Exposed

You may be sure that your sin will find you out.
Numbers 32:23

"If my kid is doing something wrong, Lord, please let him get caught."

Believe it or not, almost every parent I talked with as I began writing this book said that the "let my kids get caught" prayer—a parent's version of Numbers 32:23—was at or near the top of their list. Judging by the emails I received, we want our teens to get caught even more than we want them to finish their chores, say no to drugs, and stop wrecking the car.

I don't mind telling you I was somewhat surprised. The desire for sin to be exposed stands in stark contrast to the reality of a world in which many parents cover for their kids and do everything they can to minimize the consequences of bad decisions—whether it means staying up all night to finish a procrastinator's science project or hiring a lawyer to get charges dropped against a teen who drove home drunk.

And then there's my friend Catherine.

Catherine has younger children, and she had never heard the "let them get caught" prayer. When I told her I had prayed that for my kids, and that other parents did too, she looked confused. "Why don't you all just pray that your kids won't do anything wrong?" she asked.

It took me about half a second to process her question. And then I laughed. "I guess I could pray that," I said, "but it wouldn't work. Our kids are just like we are. They can't help it. They sin.

"And," I continued, warming to my topic, "Proverbs 28:13 says, 'Whoever conceals their sins does not prosper, but the one who confesses and renounces them finds mercy.'"

PRAYER PRINCIPLE

Concealing sin never ends well, but
confession leads to mercy.

If Catherine thought I was nuts, she had the grace not to say so. But another friend, Sharon, would have appreciated my Bible quoting. She knows it's a mercy to be found out. Still, though, she says she hates to pray the "let them get caught" prayer because it's one that God always answers.

One night, for example, her teen son kissed a girl, figuring Sharon would never know. Unbeknownst to the young Romeo, the girl went home and emailed all the details to her older sister, who forwarded the missive to one of her best friends—who just happened to be Sharon's oldest daughter! Within twenty-four hours, the email had made its way to Sharon's in-box—and "Romeo" found himself with some explaining to do!

I'm no Pew Research Center, but according to my very unscientific calculations, pretty much every teen has done something wrong. If you are one of those parents who has prayed the "let them get caught" prayer, my guess is that God has been faithful to answer it. But if you haven't tried this one yet, consider yourself warned . . .

~ ~ ~

"Honey, are you ready to go? The game starts in forty-five minutes."

Living in a college town, Sally and her husband, Rob, had become ardent fans of the university's athletic program. They had season tickets for football and basketball and almost never missed a home game. In addition to providing some good, clean entertainment, attending the games—and cheering their heads off—provided a way for Sally and Rob to connect with their teens, who loved sports every bit as much as they did. Having just sent her older daughter off to college, Sally was all too aware that Allison, their tenth-grader, would soon be gone, and she wanted to make the most of the remaining time they had together.

"Just a second, Rob," Sally replied. "I think there's something wrong with the dishwasher."

Sure enough, the appliance was overflowing—and with the clock ticking down to tip-off, a decision had to be made. "I'll call the plumber," Sally volunteered. "You and Allison go on ahead. I'll try to meet up with you at halftime."

Fortunately, the plumber was nearby. He quickly fixed the problem, and Sally followed him out to the driveway, thinking that if she hurried, she might be able to catch the end of the game.

Her thoughts were interrupted, however, when her next-door neighbor, Ben, came out to quiet his dog.

"Sorry about the barking," Ben said. "I guess Trixie just wanted us to know that you had a repairman here."

"That's okay," Sally answered. "I appreciate knowing she's on patrol."

"Well, speaking of being on patrol," Ben began, "I didn't want to say anything, but I think there's something you need to know."

Sally felt her heart skip a beat. She and Rob had just returned from a long weekend away—had there been a burglary in the neighborhood?

"I hate to be the one to tell you this, but while you were gone, Allison had some friends over."

"What? How many friends?" Sally hoped she hadn't heard correctly. Allison had been staying with a young Christian couple who had agreed to host her for the weekend. She wasn't supposed to be at home while Rob and Sally were gone.

"I don't know—maybe a hundred or so."

"What!"

"I don't think she meant for it to get out of hand. Allison is a good girl. We offered to help her get rid of everyone, but she said she could handle it."

"Uh-huh," Sally said, her thoughts now far from the basketball game. "Well, thanks for telling me."

Later that night, when Rob and Allison came home, Sally confronted her daughter with what she had learned. The story spilled out—and the longer it got, the worse it became.

Sally and Rob had given Allison permission to spend the night at a girlfriend's house one of the nights they were gone. Instead of going there, the girls decided it would be more fun to invite a few friends to gather at Allison's house. Thanks to the teen text network, what began as a small get-together quickly turned into a full-fledged bash, attracting a huge crowd of boys and girls, many of whom were drinking and smoking. Several girls wound up spending the night at Allison's house—without any adult supervision and without their parents' knowledge.

Sally felt sick to her stomach. In addition to betraying her parents' trust, Allison had deceived her babysitters, endangered her friends, and compromised her own integrity. Everyone in the community knew that Sally and Rob were Christians—what sort of message did it send when one of the biggest, baddest parties of the year was at their house?

"It was awful," Sally said later as she shared the story with me. "Of course, Allison was grounded. And she had to go to the parents of all the girls who had spent the night at our house and write them a letter to apologize for initiating the get-together and for being complicit in the deception. When she finally woke up to the fact that she had put her girlfriends' reputations—and even their lives—in danger, she truly felt terrible. It was a learning experience, to say the least."

When I asked Sally if I could use her story in this book, she got Allison's permission before saying yes. While neither of them want to dwell on the mistakes that were made, both mother and daughter acknowledge that, thanks to God's grace, what started out as a very bad choice turned into an opportunity for learning, growing, and changing.

"Had our dishwasher not started overflowing," Sally said, "who knows when—or even if—we would have found out about the party. But one thing I can say for certain is that if you pray for your teen to be found out when they do something they shouldn't—when they break the rules, lie, drink, or go somewhere they shouldn't—it is amazing how faithfully God answers that prayer.

"And," Sally concluded, "even though it's sometimes incredibly painful to discover your teen's transgressions and have to deal with the consequences, it is *so* much better than never knowing."

Poised for Prayer

As you might imagine, it wasn't easy for Sally to share her story with me. Nobody wants to talk about the big bloopers in their family. But I'm grateful for her honesty and candor, because there is so much about her story that can fill us with hope. I hope you saw what I saw.

For one thing, Sally and her husband are godly parents. Their love for the Lord colors pretty much everything about their family life, and if you didn't know better, you might think they look pretty perfect. But they're not. And if you look around at families in your church and think that other people "have it all together," think again. Everybody struggles. We *all* fall short.

Next, did you notice what Sally and Rob did when God answered their prayers? When Allison got caught, they didn't try to cover her sin or blame someone else. It would have been easy to point the finger at the kids who "crashed" Allison's party, but Sally and Rob didn't go there. Instead, they held their daughter accountable, using the experience as a teaching tool for lessons about personal responsibility and the importance of confession. We can learn from their example as we deal openly with our kids' mistakes and see them as opportunities for growth.

PRAYER PRINCIPLE

When you ask God to let your kids get
caught, be prepared for him to answer—and
trust him to bring growth in the process.

And finally, their story underscores the beauty of God's faithfulness and grace. When we ask him to let our kids get caught, we can do so knowing he isn't going to hang them out to dry. He loves them way too much for that. He will let them get caught—but he will also catch them as they fall. God is in the restoration business, and as parents, we can work hand in hand with him to get our teens back on their feet.

Remember Joseph—the guy with the technicolor dreamcoat? He was a teen when his brothers sold him into slavery and faked his death. Years later, after Joseph grew up and masterminded one of history's most successful disaster relief programs, he confronted his siblings. Instead of harboring bitterness and anger, though, he pointed to the evidence of God's handiwork. "You intended to harm me," Joseph said to his brothers in Genesis 50:20, "but God intended it for good to accomplish what is now being done, the saving of many lives."

When our kids do bad things—and they will—let's not give in to fear or discouragement. Instead, let's adjust our perspective and look for God's fingerprints, trusting in his promise to take even the darkest situation and use it to bring about something good.

Prayers You Can Use

Heavenly Father . . .

You see everything that _____ does. Open my eyes to the things I need to see, and give me the wisdom and the courage to deal with the situation when my teen is caught doing wrong.

Proverbs 15:3

_____'s sins—even the secret ones—are revealed in the light of your presence. Teach _____ to make the most of this time and grow in wisdom. *Psalm 90:8, 12*

Cause _____ to renounce secret and shameful ways. Do not let them use deception or do anything to distort your word.

2 Corinthians 4:2

Let _____ have nothing to do with the fruitless deeds of darkness, but rather expose them, realizing it is shameful even to mention what the disobedient do in secret.

Ephesians 5:11–12

When _____ is caught in sin, have mercy. Wash away all iniquity and cleanse them from sin, giving them a clean heart and a spirit that is willing to obey you. *Psalm 51:1–2, 10–12.*

Lord, if you kept a record of our sins, who could ever survive? Prompt _____ to take hold of the forgiveness you offer and learn to fear you and put their hope in your word.

Psalm 130:3–5

Repay _____ for the years that the locusts have eaten; may they praise you and never again be shamed.

Joel 2:25–26

When _____ thinks that the darkness will hide them, remind them that darkness is as light to you. Search _____ and know their heart. Turn your spotlight on any offensive words, thoughts, or behaviors, and lead them in the way everlasting.

Psalm 139:11–12, 23–24

Let _____ look to you and be radiant with a face that is never covered with shame.

Psalm 34:5

Show _____ that they are your own possession, called to show others the goodness of God. May _____ keep away from worldly desires and live properly among unbelieving neighbors so that they will see their honorable behavior and give glory to God.

1 Peter 2:9–12 NLT

In a world where many teens hate the light because they want to sin in the darkness, cause _____ to do what is right and come into the light so that others can see they are doing what you want.

John 3:20–21

Remind _____ that their sin will find them out.

Numbers 32:23

Whoever conceals sin does not prosper; prompt _____ to confess and renounce sin and find mercy.

Proverbs 28:13

Part 5

Praying about Everything

Chapter 21

Praying about Choice of Music

It is better to heed the rebuke of a wise person than to listen to the song of fools.
Ecclesiastes 7:5

One of my favorite possessions, when I was a teen, was my Sony Walkman. I'd pop in a cassette tape, adjust the headpiece so the sponges on the headphones covered my ears, and head out for a run. The music lifted my spirits.

But it had the opposite effect on my grandmother.

Gammy would start shaking her head and muttering the minute she saw me. Never mind that I was probably listening to Amy Grant or some other Christian artist; the way Gammy saw it, nothing good could come out of that newfangled device. The fact that nobody else could hear what I was listening to only fueled her suspicions. As her oldest grandchild, I was clearly headed for trouble.

Back then, I thought my grandmother was a little bit nuts. Now, though, I find myself sharing her concerns. I didn't need a Google search to tell me the power that music has over teen behavior (for better or worse), or that lyrics, as one expert put it, "tell us how to behave." I was, however, surprised to learn that the neural connectivity in our brains "hardens" by the time we hit our mid-twenties, meaning that our taste in music—and indeed, the worldview that music helps shape—is pretty much established by then.[1]

So what are our kids listening to?

If you're like me, you might not be able to decipher the lyrics in the songs that they like—or if you can figure out the actual words, you might not know what they mean. But if you're like my much cooler friend, Lisa (who is a fan of surfing, running, and professional sports), you probably do. Lisa and her husband, Chris, know all the popular bands, and when their son Michael formed a garage band with some of his buddies, she was all for it.

At first.

As the group began rehearsing, Lisa found herself increasingly concerned with some of their song choices. She knew how much the camaraderie with the other musicians meant to her son, and she didn't want to build a wall between them over what might be simply a matter of taste. Was Michael's music dangerous? Lisa didn't know, but she decided to pray about it anyway. And, as cheesy as this story sounds, it really happened . . .

ᖇ ᖇ ᖇ

Lisa's eyes were on the road, but she could sense her sixteen-year-old son's mocking attitude as she turned up the volume on her car radio. She loved contemporary Christian music, and she knew the words to almost every song her favorite station played. She was well aware that her kids preferred rock and jazz, but on days like today, when she was in the driver's seat, she kept the dial tuned to what she called "the good stuff."

"Aw, Mom," Michael groaned, "don't you get enough of this kind of music on Sundays? You are way too into church. Can't we just listen to normal music like normal people do?"

Lisa pulled into a parking spot and turned to smile at her son. "When you drive, you can listen to what you want. Now come on—let's get that hair cut. With the way it looks right now, I can't even tell if you *are* a normal person."

Walking into the salon, Lisa recalled a verse she had prayed earlier with her weekly Moms in Prayer group: "Lord, give Michael knowledge and insight so he can discern what is best and be pure and blameless" (Philippians 1:9–10). Thinking of these words, she breathed a silent prayer for his taste in music. She looked up as their favorite hairdresser, Jean Marie, approached.

"Hey, Michael," Jean Marie teased, "looks like you've been saving your hair up for me!"

"Yeah, I guess it's been a while," Michael said dryly. Jean Marie, Lisa knew, had a way of getting Michael to part with his hair and be happy about it—and looking at the pretty hairdresser, dressed in jeans and a T-shirt that showed her twentysomething figure to good advantage, Lisa had to admit a teen boy would have to be blind to not want to get his hair cut by her.

"So are you still playing guitar with that band?" Jean Marie asked as she combed Michael's hair.

"Yeah," Michael replied.

"Do you play any Christian rock?"

Lisa's ears perked up. Could it be that this goddess of a hairdresser liked Christian music?

"Christian rock?" Michael scoffed. "There's no such thing. That's an oxymoron!"

"No way!" Jean Marie countered, snipping away. "You don't have to get in the *gutter* to rock out and enjoy some good music. You can rock out to the Spirit!" Michael didn't say anything, and Lisa wondered what he was thinking. But Jean Marie wasn't finished. "You know," she added, "I think there's nothing sexier than a man who loves Jesus."

Lisa nearly dropped the magazine she was holding. Michael, however, did not flinch—which, Lisa realized, was a good thing. Jean Marie's scissors did not look very forgiving.

"What makes you find Christian guys so appealing?" Lisa prompted, hoping that Michael was listening as closely as she was.

"Well," Jean Marie began, "they have an inner confidence—the kind that comes from the heart. It's so much more attractive than the insecurity or outward arrogance so many guys have. When a man knows who he is in Christ, it shows in the way he treats people, in the things he does, and in the things he says. He has a genuine confidence—and girls like that."

Lisa turned her head so that Michael wouldn't see her smile. How very like God to put a beautiful young woman smack-dab in front of her son to deliver a message in a way no mother ever could. And the best part, Lisa thought to herself, was that since Michael's hair was two inches shorter on one side than on the other, he couldn't just get up and walk away!

> ─────── PRAYER PRINCIPLE ───────
>
> Ask God to bring people into your teen's
> life who can teach the lessons they
> may not want to hear from you.

As a mother of teens whose musical preferences are often jaw-droppingly different from my own, I could relate to Lisa's desire to see her kids start listening to "the good stuff." I also wanted my kids to have discernment when it came to choosing which lyrics, melodies, and rhythms they'd invite into their minds. As study after study confirms, music has the power to shape emotions, belief systems, and behavior, and I wanted those influences to be positive ones.

I wanted all of that—wisdom and discernment, uplifting lyrics, and music that shaped my kids' lives for good. And when we bought one of our daughters an iPod (remember those?) for Christmas one year, I counted on my husband, Robbie (who is both musically literate and technologically savvy), to keep tabs on her playlists.

He did, but not right away—and not before both of us noticed a marked downturn in our girl's countenance. With three teen daughters under our roof, Robbie and I were no strangers to mood swings, but after two weeks of what can only be described as a "funk," we began to wonder if there was a connection between our daughter's sullenness and the wires that seemed to be permanently attached to her ears. Robbie asked her to hand over the iPod.

Sure enough, there were a handful of songs—several that were very popular among her classmates—that had some pretty negative messages. When Robbie shared his concerns, our daughter (thank you, God!) agreed to delete the offensive songs. Almost overnight, it seemed as though the sunshine came out in our family again.

Coincidence? Maybe.

But maybe not.

Poised for Prayer

Author Ty Saltzgiver spent forty years getting to know—and love—teens through his work with Young Life. "Music," he says, "is really, really important. It shapes a kid. It's a doorway into their heart."

As I considered Ty's words, I thought about Paul's request. "Pray for us," he asked the Colossians, "that God may open a door for our message, so that we may proclaim the mystery of Christ."[2] I thought about Jesus, standing at the door of our hearts and knocking, awaiting an invitation to enter.[3] And I thought about the wisdom of Proverbs: "Above all else, guard your heart, for everything you do flows from it."[4]

PRAYER PRINCIPLE

Ask God to guard your teen's heart;
everything flows from it.

Our teens' hearts *are* a doorway—for good things and bad. Two forces are at work in their lives—the Holy Spirit and their sinful nature—and they are "constantly fighting each other."[5] As we try to discern which music is "bad" and what is simply "different" (as in, not that appealing to us), it can help to have a litmus test.

I am sure there are plenty of questions we might ask, but mine is fairly simple: *Does the music glorify God—or does it put the spotlight on self?* Put another way, *Does the music promote pure and noble thoughts—or does it encourage sensuality, anger, materialism, physical pleasure, or other self-centered cravings?*

Talk with your teens about the songs they like. Find out what's on their playlists. Teach them to look for messages in the songs, and give them a litmus test they can use. You may find yourself talking to a wall—my headshaking grandmother certainly did—but that's okay. When we can't talk to our kids, we can still talk to God.

God says he "bends down to listen."[6] Let's ask him to listen to the deepest longings of our teens' hearts and to open a door for the music and messages he wants them to hear. And as we pray, let's join our voices with David and ask God to lift our teens out of any "slimy pit" of music they might be into and put "a new song" in their mouths.[7]

Prayers You Can Use

Heavenly Father . . .

As _____ listens to or plays music, may they do it for your glory.   *1 Corinthians 10:31*

Draw _____ into true fellowship with you, teaching them to listen to music that brings light instead of darkness.
                                                                1 John 1:5

Teach _____ to steer clear of any music that smacks of sexual impurity or obscenity, choosing instead to sing and make music in their heart to you.   *Ephesians 5:3–4, 19*

Help _____ tune their ear to wisdom and concentrate on understanding the message behind the songs they hear.
                                                                Proverbs 2:2

Strengthen _____ so that when others refuse to put up with sound doctrine and decide to listen to the music that says what their itching ears want to hear, their ears will stay tuned to the truth.   *2 Timothy 4:3–4*

Let _____ sing for joy and worship you with a heart that hears your voice.   *Psalm 95:1–7*

In a generation that has closed its ears and finds your word offensive, prompt _____ to open their ears and listen to you.

Jeremiah 6:10

May _____ sing praise to you as long as they live.

Psalm 104:33

Don't let _____ listen to the songs of fools; instead, may they heed the rebuke of a wise person.

Ecclesiastes 7:5

Teach _____ to pray in the spirit with understanding and to sing in the spirit with understanding.

1 Corinthians 14:15 NLT

Whether _____ turns to the right or to the left, be the voice in their ears showing them exactly which way to walk—even in the aisles of an online music store.

Isaiah 30:21

Lead _____ by the Holy Spirit. Let _____ reject music that promotes sexual immorality, impure thoughts, hostility, angry outbursts, selfish ambition, and other sinful desires, choosing instead to value music that promotes genuine love, peace, kindness, and self-control.

Galatians 5:16–22

Show _____ that the world and its music—which is filled with lust, greed, and pride—will fade away, but the one who does the will of God will live forever.   *1 John 2:15–17*

Shield _____ from vulgar and violent music; instead, let the loud noises of singing, shouting, and blasting horns that they hear come from songs of joy. *Psalm 98:4–6*

Protect _____'s physical and spiritual hearing; give _____ ears to hear what your Spirit says.

Revelation 2:7

Let _____ choose music that promotes life, listening to your voice and holding fast to you.

Deuteronomy 30:19–20

May _____'s music choices reflect that which is true, honorable, right, pure, lovely, and admirable—music that is excellent and worthy of praise. *Philippians 4:8 NLT*

Chapter 22

Praying about Your Teen's Attire

Your beauty should not come from outward adornment, such as . . . the wearing of gold jewelry or fine clothes. Rather, it should be that of your inner self, the unfading beauty of a gentle and quiet spirit, which is of great worth in God's sight

1 Peter 3:3–4

Three teen girls once lived in our house. They shared the same gene pool, but when it came to getting dressed in the morning, you would have thought they had come from different planets.

One daughter chose classic, somewhat unremarkable clothing—solid color tops paired with solid color skirts or slacks. Her low-risk fashion strategy meant she was almost never late to breakfast, and—unlike her three siblings—she never once got cited for a dress code violation at school.

Another daughter liked to accessorize her outfits, choosing the entire ensemble before she went to bed each night—complete with shoes, belts, jewelry, and hair ribbons, all arranged in the way they would look on her body. Walking into her darkened room, I found myself startled by her artistry more than once. If I hadn't known better, I would have sworn she had a corpse on the floor.

The third daughter—and I am purposely not telling you who's who—got dressed every day like she'd been given two minutes to evacuate. The clothing flew everywhere as she tried on five or six different outfits before breakfast—and another two or three after it. Looking at the carnage that spewed from her closet, I was often tempted to call in a FEMA crew.

I marveled at my daughters and their different approaches to fashion, but I have to admit I often struggled—and still struggle—with the "what to wear" question. Weighing factors like comfort versus style, as well as the need to consider how an outfit could impact other people (more on that in a minute) can complicate what on the surface should not be that big an issue. And this isn't just a girl thing; apparently, even the disciples spent some time wondering about their clothing. I love the fact that Jesus deemed their concerns important enough to address—and that he gave them some straightforward advice:

> "I tell you not to worry about everyday life—whether you have enough food to eat or enough clothes to wear. For life is more than food, and your body more than clothing. . . .
>
> "Look at the lilies and how they grow. They don't work or make their clothing, yet Solomon in all his glory was not dressed as beautifully as they are. And if God cares so wonderfully for flowers that are here today and thrown into the fire tomorrow, he will certainly care for you."
>
> Luke 12:22–23, 27–28 NLT

Wouldn't it be great if we could get our teens—and for that matter, ourselves—to take the Lord's words to heart? Imagine knowing that the prom or a party was coming up and being able to trust God to provide the perfect dress. That's exactly what happened to a mom named Laurie, shortly after her family moved from the Seattle area to a new home in Iowa . . .

Laurie heard the front door open. Closing the document on her computer, she turned to see her fifteen-year-old daughter, Aimee, put her book bag on the kitchen table. From the way her teen was standing, Laurie could tell something was wrong. She knew that, as a new student, Aimee was still looking for ways to forge relationships with the other kids, and she hoped nothing had happened to make Aimee feel left out.

"How was school today?" she prompted.

"Fine. But you know the dinner the church is hosting on Saturday night?"

"Uh-huh."

"All the girls are getting together at Stacy's house to get dressed beforehand. They invited me to come over and get ready with them."

Right away, Laurie understood Aimee's concern. The dinner was to be a formal affair, and Aimee—having never been to a formal anything—had nothing to wear. Not wanting to spend a lot of money on a dress that would probably be worn only once, Laurie had emailed several friends to see whether they had something her daughter might be able to borrow. So far, though, she had come up empty. And with the dinner just three days away, she knew they were running out of time.

Even if someone did have a dress to lend, the odds were slim that it would fit Aimee's figure in an attractive way. Laurie was no prude, but she didn't want her daughter going to a church-sponsored event in one of the scanty dresses that seemed to be so popular with the teen crowd. Not only that, but Aimee's coloring—green eyes, auburn hair, and porcelain skin—left her with a limited palette when it came to the colors she found herself eager to wear.

For a teen, Aimee was remarkably mature in her outlook. Never once had she complained about not having a formal dress, and she had even gone so far as to count her blessings, knowing full well that there were people in the world who had little clothing of any kind. But Laurie's heart ached for her daughter. She knew that, like many girls, Aimee didn't always feel good about her appearance, and Laurie yearned to give her what she called a "beauty boost."

"Aimee," she said, "I know God cares about even the little stuff like formal dresses. Let's ask him to send us a dress."

"Mom, the dinner is on Saturday!"

"I know that. But let's ask him anyway."

Later that night, Laurie shared her concern with the Lord. "Father God," she prayed, "I realize this formal dinner is not a monumental thing. But if Aimee is going to go, she needs a dress. Would you please send her one? I know it would encourage her faith, and if she could get together beforehand with the other girls, it would really help her adjust to our new home and feel like she has some good friends. You are so creative, God. I know you can help us."

The next morning, Laurie awoke to a blanket of white. Another Iowa snowstorm had turned their neighborhood into a winter wonderland and, Laurie realized, had left them stranded. Laurie fixed a pot of coffee and called the city, asking them to send a snowplow as soon as they could.

Holding her steaming mug, Laurie looked out the window. Suddenly, she noticed an unfamiliar car parked on the street. She realized it would be directly in the path of the snowplow. Laurie had no idea whose car it was, but, donning her heaviest coat and a pair of sturdy boots, she aimed to find out.

After knocking on several doors, Laurie found the car's owner. It belonged to the friend of a teen named Chantel, whose mother, Weiss, invited Laurie to come inside and out of the cold. Laurie told Weiss she also had a teen daughter.

"She has this big dinner tomorrow night," Laurie said. "It's at our church—but so far, Aimee has nothing to wear."

"What's the attire?" Weiss asked.

"It's supposed to be formal. Aimee has never been to anything that fancy before."

"Come upstairs," Weiss said. "I have something to show you."

Laurie followed her neighbor up the stairs and into a bedroom. Weiss opened the closet, where a single dress hung.

"That's Aimee's favorite color!" Laurie gasped. "It's gorgeous!"

The dress was a pale, shimmery sage green—just like Aimee's eyes. It hung almost all the way to the floor, and even on its hanger, Laurie could tell that the drape of the fabric was beautiful.

"Look," Weiss said, "the price tags are still attached. I bought this for Chantel, but she's never worn it. The color is just not right for her. Do you think Aimee would like it?"

Laurie knew Aimee would love the dress, but she wondered how much it had cost. When she saw the tags, though, her heart skipped a beat. Not only was the dress Aimee's exact size, but it was remarkably affordable.

"I bought it on sale a few months ago," Weiss explained. "You are welcome to it if you want it."

Carrying the dress back through the snow, Laurie wanted to laugh out loud. Long before they had ever moved to Iowa, God had known that this Saturday night would be special for Aimee. And when Aimee slipped the dress over her head, standing back to look at her reflection in the mirror, there could be no doubt: The dress was never meant to be worn by Chantel; it was intended for Aimee, the new girl in town, the one who needed to know that God loved her, that he thought she was beautiful, and that he didn't want her to worry about what she would wear.

PRAYER PRINCIPLE

God loves your teen, and he cares about
even the smallest details in their lives.

Poised for Prayer

I love knowing that God cares about something as seemingly inconsequential as clothing. And the Bible is full of fashion commentary. Consider, for example, the women of Zion. They wore headbands, necklaces, earrings, bracelets, and veils. They adorned themselves with anklets, sashes, headdresses, and charms and put rings on their fingers and through their noses. They carried perfume bottles, purses, and mirrors. They wore tiaras and shawls. And over it all, they put on fine robes, capes, and cloaks.[1]

(And I thought *we* were short on closet space!)

The ladies of Zion may have looked fantastic, but God saw beyond the bangles. He says they were "haughty, walking along with outstretched necks, flirting with their eyes, strutting along with swaying hips, with ornaments jingling on their ankles." God saw their proud, rebellious hearts—and in response, he vowed to put sores on their heads and make them go bald.[2] Now there's a story you won't read in the pages of *Vogue*!

That's just one of many places where the Bible links clothing with character. I'm not sure how much the apostle Paul knew about fashion, but he certainly saw the connection between what we wear and what we value, or who we are:

- "Clothe yourselves with the Lord Jesus Christ," he said, "and do not think about how to gratify the desires of the flesh."[3] *Translation: If your aim is to please God, don't wear something that fuels things like pride, greed, envy, or lust.*
- "Don't copy the behavior and customs of this world."[4] *Translation: Just because "everyone" dresses like that doesn't mean we should.*
- Or how about this one from Paul's letter to Timothy: "I also want the women to dress modestly, with decency and propriety, adorning themselves, not with elaborate hairstyles or gold or pearls or expensive clothes, but with good deeds, appropriate for women who profess to worship God."[5] *Translation: Your attention should be devoted to godly deeds, not to the way you look.*

I once served on a committee tasked with educating students about sexual harassment. I remember coming home from a meeting and telling my daughters that while they should absolutely expect their male peers to respect them, they also bore responsibility for creating a climate of honor. "Men are visual," I said, "and that gives women power. Out of respect for the guys you know, you should not abuse that power by dressing in a way that will make them struggle or sin."

Politically correct? Probably not. But honoring people by the way we dress is not just a guy-girl issue; it's a Philippians 2 issue, one where God tells us to value other people above ourselves, looking not to our own interests but to theirs.[6]

PRAYER PRINCIPLE

Ask God to help your teens honor
others by the way they dress.

Whether it's a bra that is designed to be seen, boxer shorts that (as a group of teen boys told me) send a message about male "identity" (plaid apparently signifies something very different than plain), or the blue jeans that my grandmother didn't want me to wear out to dinner because of how "disrespectful" they were, our clothing choices impact other people. And in a culture that teaches kids to dress in a way that says, "Look at me!" it can be hard to turn the tables and say, "Look out for others."

And yet that's exactly what God wants us to do.

"Make up your mind," he says, "not to put any stumbling block or obstacle in the way of a brother or sister." If something we eat, drink, or wear causes distress, we are "no longer acting in love."[7]

Instead of conforming to the pattern of the world and wearing clothing designed to garner attention or peer approval, let's ask God to transform our perspective—and our kids' perspective, renewing our minds so that our clothing choices will line up with his will—his "good, pleasing and perfect will."[8]

Let's pray that God will open our eyes to see the clothing of our culture the way he sees it. And because parents and teens often have very different perspectives on style (what says "inappropriate" to us may say "artistic" to them), let's also ask for divine discernment so we can spot the difference between clothing that is merely *unusual* (and not worth arguing over) and that which is *immodest*. Most of all, let's ask the Lord to change our hearts, so that, instead of dressing to fit in with the world or draw attention to *ourselves*, we will clothe ourselves with Christ, letting all we say and do and wear shine the spotlight on *him*.

Clothing is a big deal to teens, and when we take the time to pray about what they wear—whether they simply need a dress for a dance or a full-scale attitude adjustment in the "Look at me!" department—we invite God to demonstrate his power and provision in their lives. After all, if God cares enough to outfit the lilies, we can be sure he cares about our kids.

Prayers You Can Use

Heavenly Father . . .

Clothe _____ with the Lord Jesus Christ so that they won't spend time thinking about ways to gratify the desires of the flesh.

Romans 13:14

For a daughter: Clothe _____ with strength and dignity. Help her remember that charm is deceptive, and beauty is fleeting, but a woman who fears the Lord is to be praised.

Proverbs 31:25, 30

May _____ be dressed ready for service.

Luke 12:35

Clothe _____ with your Spirit, as you did for Gideon, so they can lead others in wisdom and righteousness.

Judges 6:34

Keep _____ from dressing in such a way that could cause anyone to stumble into sin. *1 Corinthians 10:32*

Let _____ be content with the clothing they have, with plenty or little. *Philippians 4:12 NLT*

Let _____'s attractiveness come from good deeds rather than from any elaborate hairstyles or expensive clothing.

1 Timothy 2:9–10

Clothe _____ with joy, with a heart that sings to you.

Psalm 30:11–12

Don't let _____ be like a haughty woman of Zion, walking around with an outstretched neck and flirtatious eyes. Instead, may _____ be clothed with humility, knowing that you oppose the proud but give grace to the humble.

Isaiah 3:16; 1 Peter 5:5

Whether _____ needs sports equipment, school clothing, new shoes, or even a gown or a tuxedo, help them rely on you, knowing that you promise to meet all of our needs according to your glorious riches in Christ Jesus.

Philippians 4:19

Help _____ not to worry about clothing. Point their eyes toward your creation and how you clothe even the grass of the field with beauty.

Matthew 6:28–30

Crown _____ with your beauty, removing any spirit of despair and replacing it with a garment of praise.

Isaiah 61:3

Don't let _____ dress to impress others; rather, cause them to respect others and look out for their interests.

Philippians 2:3–4 NLT

Clothe _____ with the belt of truth, the body armor of your righteousness, shoes that are ready to preach the good news of peace, and the shield of faith to stop Satan's fiery arrows. Outfit _____ with the helmet of salvation and the sword of the Spirit, which is your word.   *Ephesians 6:14–17 NLT*

Chapter 23

Praying for Your Teen Athlete

Everyone who competes in the games goes into strict training. They do it to get a crown that will not last; but we do it to get a crown that will last forever.

1 Corinthians 9:25

Many of my prayer partners have children who play sports. While the giftedness of each individual athlete varies widely—we've prayed for state champions as well as for perennial benchwarmers—we moms share many common concerns.

We want our kids to be men and women of character. Half the reason I signed my kids up for soccer when they were barely out of diapers was that I had heard that sports develop things like self-discipline, perseverance, and a willingness to sacrifice your own interests for the good of a team.

We want our kids to grow up healthy and strong. One of my friends reported that, after listening to her pray one day, her son said, "Mom, as long as you're praying that I will get to be five foot ten, why don't you just go ahead and make it six feet?"

And perhaps more than anything—at least from the vantage

point of the sidelines during the heat of competition—we want our kids to be safe. Robbie was only ten years old when he started coming out of football and lacrosse games with more bruises than a late-season peach, and I realized—duh!—that he really could get hurt out there. Shoulder pads were fine, but I didn't want him to take the field unless he was also covered in prayer!

Psalm 121:3 promises that the God who watches over us will "neither slumber nor sleep." He is always on watch. And unlike the parents who sit next to me in the stands, God never misses one of the plays. His view is unobstructed; his attention is focused; and—as Jesus reminds us in Matthew 6:8—he knows exactly what our teens need, even before we ask him.

My friend Kenzie is raising two very athletic boys. Her son Trey began winning road races in elementary school, crossing the finish line with enough time to suck down a Gatorade before the next challenger even came into view, and I wasn't the least bit surprised when Trey was offered a spot on the track team at the University of Virginia.

For Kenzie's other son, Duncan, the athletic road was not quite as smooth. Like all the praying moms I know, Kenzie routinely asks God to protect her kids—but what she discovered is that God's idea of keeping a teen safe doesn't come with all the padding a mom thinks it should . . .

℃ ℃ ℃

By the time Duncan was in middle school, it was obvious he was going to be a big guy. He shot past his mom, his dad, and his older brother, Trey—and much to the delight of area coaches, he developed a passion for football. He enrolled in a junior NFL camp, never once complaining about the heat, the rigorous practice schedule, or the endless hits he took. One day, after a particularly rough play, Duncan tried to get up and discovered he couldn't walk. "Coach," he said calmly, "I think I hurt my knee."

Duncan, at age fourteen, had broken his left femur. Three screws in his leg and an entire summer filled with rehab left him eager to get back into the game, and when school started again in the fall, the high school coaches were equally ready to see him back on the field. Duncan soon found himself in the starting lineup, calling the plays for the team.

"Can you believe it?" Kenzie said to her husband, Will, as they watched their freshman son from the stands. "He's having the time of his life!"

Suddenly, though, Kenzie's delight turned to concern. A player had gone down. Scanning the field and then the sidelines for Duncan's jersey, Kenzie turned her attention back to the field just as the downed player's helmet was removed. Kenzie grabbed Will's arm in disbelief. It was Duncan.

This time, he couldn't move. Kenzie and Will raced onto the field, along with a host of coaches and trainers. It was obvious that Duncan had broken his other leg—and that this break was much worse than the first. With his head in Will's lap, Duncan cried out in agony, and then, in the hour that it took for the ambulance to locate the football field, he struggled to maintain consciousness. "Hang on, Dunc," Will urged, silently willing the paramedics to hurry.

When they finally got Duncan to the hospital, doctors put four more pins into his body—this time into his right leg. *Here we go again*, Kenzie thought to herself, dreading the months of rehab that undoubtedly lay ahead. Duncan, she knew, would hate being sidelined during his freshman season.

But sitting on the sidelines turned out to be the least of Duncan's worries. Three days after coming home from the hospital, he began to have trouble breathing. "We need to get you checked out," Kenzie said, struggling to keep the concern out of her voice as they drove the all-too-familiar route to the hospital.

Duncan, the doctors discovered, had a life-threatening pulmonary embolism.

At this point, I need to interrupt the story to tell you that, when it comes to trusting God, Kenzie is probably the most steadfast woman I know. Several years ago, when a medical resident (mistakenly, it turned out) thought that Kenzie had breast cancer and began to cry in the examining room, Kenzie was the one who refused to be shaken. "You need to pull yourself together!" she admonished the distraught young doctor. "It's going to be all right—but you will *never* be able to help your patients if you act like this!"

That steadfastness turned out to be critical as Kenzie and Will spent the next six days by Duncan's side, watching him wage a life-and-death battle to breathe. Her eyes on the monitors, Kenzie learned to count respirations and heartbeats by the minute. When the time came to remove Duncan's cast in an attempt to find the source of the embolism—a procedure that was guaranteed to be both frightening and painful—she retreated to the hallway to pray, leaving Will to stay by Duncan's side.

Tears streaming down her face, Kenzie fell to the floor to intercede for her son. She cried out to the Lord—and then without warning, she heard his voice in reply: *This will be a pivotal time in Duncan's life.* To Kenzie, *pivotal* meant that Duncan's injury would mark a turning point in his life—and that he would not die.

Duncan spent the next six days in the hospital and was put on a blood thinner to prevent additional clotting. Kenzie suspected he would return to school in a wheelchair, and when the doctor insisted that he use crutches instead, she blanched. In her mind, the opportunity for additional injury was far greater for a boy on crutches than for one safely ensconced in a chair. She understood the doctor's concern—that the use of a wheelchair could lead to a permanent lack of mobility in Duncan's knee—but her mother's intuition told her that crutches were a bad idea.

Sure enough, Duncan had only been back at school for a few days when he slipped on a wet tile floor as he tried to open a door, rebreaking his femur. Doctors set the bone again and sent Duncan home to recover—only this time the pain did not subside. He seemed to be slipping away.

A call to the orthopedic surgeon netted a prescription for painkillers, which Will hurried to the pharmacy to fetch. Sitting by her son's bedside, Kenzie asked if there was anything else she could do. "Mom," Duncan pleaded, "please just pray!"

Kenzie did—and heard God's voice a second time: *Don't mask this pain.* She realized that Duncan was going into shock—he had clammy skin, a rapid pulse, and eyes that could not focus—and that drugs were not what he needed. She called 911.

Back at the hospital, they learned that Duncan was bleeding internally. His leg—and his life—was in serious danger. Doctors scheduled another operation, which they warned Duncan might not survive. "Lord," Kenzie prayed, "you said this would be a pivotal time in Duncan's life. All I can do is pray. Save him, God."

The surgery was successful. The bleeding stopped, and from that point on, Duncan began to improve. He moved from his bed and then to his wheelchair—which his buddies had customized with everything from flags and pinwheels to cushions and a cup holder—and then to the physical therapist's office.

A year later, Duncan was wrestling on the varsity squad.

He still bears the scars from his ordeal—both on his legs and in his memory. Likewise, Kenzie still cries sometimes when she talks about her son's brush with death. But what moves her to tears even more is the tender way God cared for their family, drawing close in their darkest moments to reassure them of his presence. He showed them, as God showed the Israelites in Joshua 1:9, how to be strong and courageous rather than terrified or discouraged—because he was with them, no matter what.

"I don't know why God allowed Duncan to get hurt," Kenzie says, "but I know he used the experience to reveal himself to us and to our boys and to teach us about the importance of prayer. Seeing Trey kneel beside Duncan's bed and pray for him, or listening to them talk and laugh when Trey would come home at night and regale Duncan with the goings-on in the teen world, watching them grow closer to each other and to the Lord—those are the images I will remember. As difficult as it was, Duncan's injury is not, first and foremost, a painful memory. It is an amazing testimony of God's love."

PRAYER PRINCIPLE

When we realize that God is more concerned
with spiritual victories than athletic victories,
the most painful experiences often become
the most beautiful testimonies of his love.

Poised for Prayer

Listening to Kenzie's story and thinking of Duncan's courage as
he faced one medical hurdle and athletic setback after another, I
couldn't help but wonder about all the times when our prayers for
our teen's safety and protection seem to go unanswered. God *did*
spare Duncan's life, but did he have to put him on the bench—or,
more specifically, in a wheelchair or on crutches—for nearly two
years?

I asked God the same thing when our son Robbie landed a
spot on the varsity lacrosse team as a scrawny ninth-grader—and
then had his leg broken by an overzealous goalie partway through
the season. And I wondered what God was up to when my kids
played for coaches whose methods they (and I) didn't understand
or agree with. Or when the refs called them for a foul they didn't
commit. Or when they got cut from a team.

Athletics, perhaps more than any other endeavor, can be a
crucible for our teens' character and a proving ground for their
faith. And for ours too. How we respond in the face of disappointment or adversity—as well as in victory—speaks volumes
about who we are and what we believe about God.

PRAYER PRINCIPLE

God can use sports to shape and refine
a teen's character. (A parent's too.)

Scripture tells the story of three teens—strapping young men named Shadrach, Meshach, and Abednego—who found their faith tested by circumstances far more intimidating than broken bones, unfair calls, or crazy coaches. When these guys refused to play by the king's rules—bowing down to worship his ninety-foot-tall golden statue—he didn't make them run extra laps or sit out for the second half. He ordered that they be thrown into a blazing furnace.[1]

Had I been in their shoes—or more to the point, had I been one of their mothers—I would have been shocked. Angry. Terrified. I'm not sure what I would have said, but it may have started with something like, *"Excuse me, Mr. Ref!"*

But these boys took a different approach. They looked at the king and said, "If we are thrown into the blazing furnace, the God we serve is able to deliver us from it, and he will deliver us from Your Majesty's hand. But even if he does not, we want you to know, Your Majesty, that we will not serve your gods or worship the image of gold you have set up."[2]

As parents, we can learn a lot from Shadrach, Meshach, and Abednego. They trusted God completely—without reservation and to the point where their very lives were at stake. If we can do the same thing as we pray for our teen athletes—asking God to bless and protect them but recognizing that his ultimate goal is to win a spiritual victory in their lives—we can sit on the sidelines cheering—and praying—for our kids with confidence and peace.

Prayers You Can Use

Heavenly Father . . .

As the mountains surround Jerusalem, surround _____ with your protection, now and forevermore. *Psalm 125:2*

Do not let _____'s foot slip; keep them from all harm. Thank you for being a God who neither slumbers nor sleeps but watches over my teen, now and forevermore. *Psalm 121:3–8*

Help _____ run in such a way as to get the prize and value strict training—both in athletics, where the victor's crown is temporal, and in life, where the crown lasts forever.

1 Corinthians 9:24-25

Grant _____ grace to submit to coaches and referees, demonstrating humility toward everyone. *1 Peter 5:5*

When a bad call goes against _____, remind them that Jesus was crushed, oppressed, and afflicted, even though he had done nothing wrong, and he did not open his mouth.

Isaiah 53:5–7

When _____ struggles with athletic disappointment or injury, remind them of your plans to prosper them and give them hope and a future. Prompt _____ to pray, especially during seasons of discouragement, and listen to them when they call on you. *Jeremiah 29:11–12*

Use athletic trials—including injuries, lack of playing time, poor coaching, getting cut from a team—to strengthen and refine _____'s faith, proving it genuine and of greater worth than gold.   *1 Peter 1:6–7*

Help _____ to remember that opponents may be strong in the flesh, but you are with them to help fight the battles.
                                                                 2 Chronicles 32:8

Let _____ see troubles as an opportunity for great joy, since endurance grows when faith is tested. Use disappointments and defeats to make _____ perfect and complete, needing nothing.   *James 1:2–4 NLT*

Strengthen _____ when they are weary and grant power when they are weak. Cause them to hope in you; renew their strength; let them run and not grow weary and walk and not be faint.   *Isaiah 40:29–31*

As _____ runs the race of life, let them throw off everything that hinders and the sin that so easily entangles. Equip _____ to run with perseverance, keeping their eyes fixed on Jesus so they will not grow weary and lose heart.
                                                                 Hebrews 12:1–3

Help _____ not to fear but to stand firm and trust you. Whether competing on the athletic field or waging a battle against sickness or injury, may they remember that you are fighting for them.   *Exodus 14:13–14*

Command your angels concerning _____ to guard them in all their ways.   *Psalm 91:11*

May _____ be joyful in hope, patient in affliction, and faithful in prayer—whether they have a starting position or aren't getting as much playing time as they want.   *Romans 12:12*

In sports and in life, equip _____ to be on guard, to stand firm in faith, to be courageous, and to be strong.

1 Corinthians 16:13

When _____ enjoys an athletic victory or accomplishment, prompt them to give you the credit, knowing that everything they have—including athletic talent and ability—comes from your hand.   *1 Chronicles 29:12–14*

Chapter 24

Praying for Your Teen's Future (Education, Career, Marriage, and More)

*"What no eye has seen,
    what no ear has heard,
and what no human mind has conceived"—
    the things God has prepared for those who love
    him.*

1 Corinthians 2:9

I had no idea when I wrote *Praying the Scriptures for Your Children* that I would later write a book to help us pray for our teens. And I had no idea when I wrote the original edition of *Praying the Scriptures for Your Teens* that I would still be writing—and praying—when my kids hit their young adult years. Truth be told, part of me kept thinking that one day my kids would grow up, the cake would be baked, and I could sit back—for better or for worse—and say, like Jesus did, "It is finished."

That didn't happen, of course, and it never will. You never stop being a parent. And you never stop praying.

I love the picture that pastor and author Jack Hayford paints. He says that prayer is a "partnership of the redeemed child of God working hand in hand with God toward the realization of his redemptive purposes on earth."[1] As you look ahead toward your teen's future—toward their God-given purpose in life—can you think of anything more encouraging than knowing that when you pray about things like educational prospects, ministry opportunities, career choices, and your child's eventual marriage partner, you are slipping your hand into almighty God's hand and inviting him to bring about all that he has planned?

PRAYER PRINCIPLE

When we pray for our teens, we partner with God
as he accomplishes his good plans for their lives.

Obviously, there are no rules or formulas to dictate how we should pray for our teens, but I want to offer a few principles that have helped shape my own prayers for my kids' future.

When it came to their education, for instance, I asked God to place a hedge of protection around their hearts and emotions so they would not be drawn to any colleges that were not on his heavenly radar for them. I prayed that their high school guidance counselors would have wisdom and discernment and that the Lord would bring older teens and young adults into their lives to open their eyes to schools and career paths they might not have considered. I also prayed for my husband, Robbie, and me, that our preconceived ideas about colleges—everything from academic rankings to social and spiritual environments—would bow in submission to God's perspective on the subject.

In terms of careers and ministry opportunities, I love the wisdom my friend Susan offers. As we seek to prepare our kids for what lies ahead, Susan says, "God's job is to call them; our job is simply to equip them for whatever he has planned." With this goal in mind, she and her husband, John, sought to give their five children the skills and the perspectives they would need to befriend and dine with people who were experiencing homelessness or unemployment as well as business executives, political leaders, and kings. "I don't know whether God will call my kids to work in a soup kitchen or as the United States ambassador to the Court of St. James," Susan told me. "I want them to be ready—and willing—to do whatever God has planned."

As I read Susan's annual family letter one year, I couldn't help but think that it was a good thing she had parented—and prayed—the way she did. Her kids grew up, got married, and moved all over the map—including to England, where one of her sons lived just a stone's throw from the Court of St. James! Through their family lives, business pursuits, and ministry opportunities, these young adults are serving the Lord and accomplishing his purposes—drawing from a deep well of parental prayers and preparation.

PRAYER PRINCIPLE

God's job is to call our teens; our job
is to equip them to respond.

On the subject of marriage, it's never too early to start praying for your teen's eventual spouse and for their marriage itself. This arena represents a wonderful opportunity to practice praying specifically. Rather than praying that your teen will marry a particular *person*, however, allow things like *character traits* and *personal attributes* to shape your prayers.

Consider how Abraham did it.

When the time came for Isaac to marry, Abraham had some fairly concrete ideas about the type of wife he wanted for his son. She couldn't be a Canaanite; rather, he wanted someone from his own country, someone whose family acknowledged the Lord. Too old to make the journey himself, Abraham sent his servant to find a good match for his boy.

The servant stood beside a spring in Abraham's hometown and, as the young women came out to draw water, he prayed a very specific prayer:

> "May it be that when I say to a young woman, 'Please let down your jar that I may have a drink,' and she says, 'Drink, and I'll water your camels too' — let her be the one you have chosen for your servant Isaac. By this I will know that you have shown kindness to my master."
>
> Genesis 24:14

Obviously, Abraham's servant was asking God for a sign. But I think there was more to his prayer than this. I think that when he prayed for a young woman who would offer him water — and water for his camels as well (all ten of them—animals who could drink twenty-five gallons of water apiece!) — the servant was asking God to show him a young woman with the kindness, thoughtfulness, generosity, patience, and strength that Isaac would value in a wife. And indeed, Rebekah turned out to be all of these things, and more.

Over the years, I've talked with parents who've come before God with all sorts of requests regarding their child's marriage partner.

One of my friends—whose own parents divorced when she was a young girl—prays that her teens will marry men and women who come from unbroken homes. Another mom asked God to let her kids find their mates early in life, both so they can enjoy the blessing of marriage as they "grow up together" and to lessen the pressures of sexual temptation during their young adult years. And one young soccer player I know—a gal who led her team to a D-1 conference championship—told me she can't imagine marrying anyone who didn't love playing sports, so she and her parents are asking God to set her up with an athlete.

My own prayers tend to center around husbands and wives who have a passion for Christ—loving him with all their heart, soul, mind, and strength[2]—and who know the blessings and joy that accompany strong family relationships and a commitment to honoring your parents.[3] And if my kids' spouses also happen to be blessed with a good sense of humor, I'll take that too.

In all of these areas—education, career paths, ministry opportunities, and marriage—perhaps the best prayer we can pray for our teens is that God's presence will go with them. God's charge in Joshua 1:9—that the Israelites would "be strong and courageous" and not terrified or discouraged, since he had promised to be with them—can offer encouragement to a teen or a young adult as they head off on a missions trip or into a new job, but it proves an even more potent salve when applied to the heart of an anxious parent! When my twentysomething brother, David, and his young bride, Cherie, moved to China, the knowledge that God had called them there—and that he had promised to be with them—was probably the only thing that kept our families from wrapping ourselves around their ankles at the airport and begging them not to go.

Finally, when you consider your teen's future and look at his or her interests and abilities, remember the wisdom couched in 1 Samuel 16:7—that God doesn't always see things like we do. When our family took a surfing vacation in Central America, Hillary—then sixteen—didn't brush her hair for a week. She washed it, so I didn't complain; I just put it down to some sort of teen "self-expression." But then I looked around at the locals and realized that Hillary—the only one of us who speaks Spanish—blended into the laid-back culture beautifully. And when we met an American seminary graduate who holds church services in an open-air restaurant, she was entranced. Hillary loved the fellow's outreach style, and as I watched her during our trip, I found myself thanking God for the way he had put her together. With her tousled blonde hair and coconut-ringed fingers, Hillary had been equipped to go into places where hair dryer–dependent folks like me never could!

Poised for Prayer

When it comes to praying about your teen's future—whether you need wisdom in selecting the right college, peace about a chosen career path, or guidance and protection as your child leaves your nest and starts flying on their own—God's promise in Jeremiah 29:11–13 serves as a beautiful launching pad for our prayers:

> "For I know the plans I have for you," declares the LORD,
> "plans to prosper you and not to harm you, plans to give you

hope and a future. Then you will call on me and come and
pray to me, and I will listen to you. You will seek me and find
me when you seek me with all your heart."

God has specific and generous plans for our teens, and he has
vowed to listen to them and to be found by them as they press on
to know him better.

And he's promised to listen to us. I love how the New Living
Translation renders Psalm 116:2:

> Because he bends down to listen,
> I will pray as long as I have breath.

God bends down to listen. He invites us to pray—now and
always.

As your kids make the transition from the teen years to young
adulthood, you'll find more prayer topics—and more prayers—in
Praying the Scriptures for Your Adult Children, a book that covers
everyday concerns, from finding a good place to live and forging
healthy friendships to dealing with harder things like addictions,
rocky marriages, and kids who walk away from their families
and their faith. I think my favorite chapter in that book is the
one about blessing and releasing your children, loving them even
when you don't love all the choices they make.

It's never too early—or too late—to speak blessings over our
kids. The Bible is full of examples of parents who did that, from
Hannah's dedication of her young son to God at the tabernacle to
Jacob's farewell words to Joseph and his brothers.[4] In their book
The Love Dare for Parents, Stephen and Alex Kendrick explain
what a modern-day family blessing looks like. "It's a parent," they

say, "using their God-given authority to verbally affirm their children for who they are, while also encouraging and inspiring them toward future success."[5]

The words we speak carry power. "Words kill," Scripture says, "words give life; they're either poison or fruit—you choose."[6] I don't know where you are today or what decisions your family is facing, but I am confident of this: *God loves your teen, and he has a wonderful plan for their life.* As you partner with God to accomplish his good purposes through your prayers, let your teens know that. Let them know that God is for them—and that you are too.

Speak a blessing over your children.

You'll find a few Scripture-based blessings in the prayers below. One of our favorites—words we said to our kids at the breakfast table, as they went out the door, and when they tucked us into bed late at night (yes, that happened more than once during the teen years)—comes from the blessing God told Moses to speak over the Israelites. Borrow this one for your own family if you like—and as you do, know that I have prayed it for you:

> The LORD bless you
>   and keep you;
> the LORD make his face shine on you
>   and be gracious to you;
> the LORD turn his face toward you
>   and give you peace.[7]

Prayers You Can Use

Heavenly Father . . .

Let _____ be glad for all that you are planning. May _____ be joyful in hope, patient in affliction, and faithful in prayer.   *Romans 12:12*

Fulfill your purpose in _____. Give them a rich and satisfying life.   *John 10:10 NLT*

Fill _____ with knowledge and depth of insight to discern what is best in their future schooling, career choices, and family life. May _____ be pure and blameless, filled with the fruit of righteousness that comes through Jesus, so as to bring glory to your name.   *Philippians 1:9–11*

Remind _____ that you have plans to prosper them and not to harm them, plans to give them hope and a future. Cause _____ to come to you and pray about everything, knowing that you will listen.   *Jeremiah 29:11–12*

As _____ becomes more independent, teach them to trust in you with all their heart, leaning not on their own understanding but submitting to you so that you will make their paths straight.   *Proverbs 3:5–6*

When _____ faces a big decision—a career choice, a marriage partner, or something else—may they see the situation through your eyes and respond to people and circumstances with your wisdom and your love.   *1 Samuel 16:7*

Fill _____ with the knowledge of your will through all spiritual wisdom and understanding, that they may live a life worthy of you and please you in every way.   *Colossians 1:9–10*

Enable _____ to support and provide for their family, so that no one can accuse them of denying the faith.
1 Timothy 5:8

Teach _____ to manage time wisely and grow in wisdom.
Psalm 90:12

Do not let _____ be arrogant or put their hope in wealth, but cause them to trust you and be rich in good deeds, generous, and always willing to share.   *1 Timothy 6:17–18*

Place a hedge of protection around _____ and all that they have, so that nothing will harm them and they will not be drawn to anything that is not from you. Bless the work of their hands.
Job 1:10

When _____ meets and falls in love with the one they will marry, let their relationship be marked by patience, kindness, humility, selflessness, truthfulness, and joy. Let their love never fail.   *1 Corinthians 13:4–8*

Whatever _____'s hand finds to do, let them work at it with all their heart, as though they are working for you and not for human masters.   *Colossians 3:23*

Do immeasurably more in _____'s life than all we could ever ask or imagine. Display your power in their life, and may they bring glory to you for all generations.

Ephesians 3:20–21

May _____ and their descendants be known among the nations, and may all who see them acknowledge that they are a people the Lord has blessed.   *Isaiah 61:9*

Bless _____ and keep them; may your face shine on them. Turn your face toward _____ and give them peace.

Numbers 6:24–26

Acknowledgments

Imagine how you would feel if someone were to ask you all sorts of personal questions about your teen, your parenting, and your prayer life—and then took your answers and put them in a book.

Hard, right? Right. And I could not be more grateful to the moms and dads—from my dearest friends to complete strangers like the mother I met as we waited together to pick up our kids from a Christian summer camp—who were bold enough, vulnerable enough, and faith-filled enough to share their stories with me. In return for your gift, I'm asking God to throw open the floodgates of heaven and pour out so much blessing on your families that you will not be able to contain it![1]

I also want to express my deepest appreciation to the talented team of editors, designers, and marketing professionals at Zondervan—especially Carolyn McCready, Dirk Buursma, Kait Lamphere, Curt Diepenhorst, Alicia Kasen, and Andrea Kelly. Thank you for coming alongside me and a whole new generation of parents with your wisdom and expertise as we worked to expand and update this material. I love how you bring a love for God's Word to all you do; may he continue to show you his approval and make your efforts successful.[2]

And finally, to my husband, Robbie, and our four (now adult) children—Hillary, Annesley, Virginia, and Robbie—looking back on the teen years in our family's life, I marvel at God's faithfulness. Even when I couldn't see what he was doing, he was at work. And he is still at work. My prayer for you is the same today as it was years ago:

> And this is my prayer: that your love may abound more and more in knowledge and depth of insight, so that you may be able to discern what is best and may be pure and blameless for the day of Christ, filled with the fruit of righteousness that comes through Jesus Christ—to the glory and praise of God.
>
> Philippians 1:9–11

> The true purpose of prayer is that God may be glorified in the answer.
>
> R. A. Torrey, *How to Pray*

Notes

Introduction to the New Edition: Whack-a-Mole Parenting
1. John 21:25.
2. Hebrews 4:12; Isaiah 55:11; Romans 15:4.
3. Hebrews 4:12.
4. Hebrews 4:16.
5. 1 Samuel 7:7–12.
6. R. A. Torrey, *How to Pray* (Chicago: Moody, 1900), 75.
7. Colossians 4:3.
8. Psalm 79:13

Chapter 1: Praying for Your Teen's Relationship with Christ
1. Matthew 18:19–20.
2. Ephesians 3:18.
3. Ephesians 4:12.
4. Isaiah 55:11.

Chapter 2: Praying for Good Friends
1. Mark 8:38.
2. My parents didn't know it, but family experts—ranging from Dr. James Dobson to the mother of five who sits a few rows behind me at church—say that sending a teen to a Christian camp is one of the best financial investments a parent can make in a child. Two of our favorite camps are the ones run by Young Life (YoungLife.org) and Kanakuk (Kanakuk.com).

3. For more information on the Fellowship of Christian Athletes, visit the website at www.fca.org.
4. Proverbs 13:20 NLT.
5. The "hedge of protection" prayer comes from Job 1:10.
6. John 15:13–15; Deuteronomy 31:6.

Chapter 3: Praying for Connection to a Church Community

1. Romans 4:17; Philippians 1:6.
2. Romans 12:12.

Chapter 4: Praying for Dating Relationships

1. John 15:10–11 NLT.
2. Proverbs 4:23; 2 Corinthians 6:14.
3. Proverbs 21:1.

Chapter 5: Praying for Your Teen's Relationship with You

1. Paul David Tripp, *Age of Opportunity: A Biblical Guide to Parenting Teens* (Phillipsburg, NJ: P & R, 2001), 17.
2. Exodus 20:12; Leviticus 19:3; Deuteronomy 5:16; 27:16; Proverbs 1:8; 23:22; Matthew 15:4; Mark 7:10; Colossians 3:20–21; Ephesians 6:2–3.
3. Exodus 20:12; Ephesians 6:3 NLT.

Chapter 6: Praying for Honesty and Integrity

1. Jeremiah 9:4–6 NLT.
2. Genesis 4:8–10 TLB.
3. Exodus 20:16; Revelation 21:8.
4. See, for instance, Psalm 5:6; Proverbs 6:16–17; 12:22.
5. John 8:44.
6. Genesis 27; 29:16–25; Acts 5:1–10.
7. Philippians 1:6.

Notes

Chapter 7: Praying for an Others-Centered Outlook

1. Joe White and Jim Weidmann, ed., *Parents' Guide to the Spiritual Mentoring of Teens* (Wheaton, IL: Tyndale, 2001), 401.
2. For more information on the Kanakuk experience, see Kanakuk.com.
3. Galatians 5:22–23 lists all the fruit of the Spirit.
4. Philippians 4:6 TLB.

Chapter 8: Praying for a Humble, Teachable Heart

1. Isaiah 55:8.
2. Numbers 12:3.
3. Daniel 4:28–37.
4. John 1:19–34.
5. Psalm 147:11 NLT; Ephesians 3:20.

Chapter 9: Praying through Anger to Composure

1. 1 Chronicles 28:9.
2. Matthew 4:19; John 21:19.
3. Matthew 16:22; 26:74; John 18:11.
4. 1 Peter 1:13; 2:17, 19–20; 3:9.
5. 1 Peter 2:21.

Chapter 10: Praying for Compassion and Kindness

1. For more information on Moms in Prayer, visit the website at www.momsinprayer.org.

Chapter 11: Praying for Your Teen Driver

1. See NHTSA.gov for statistics on teen driving and recommended rules that parents can set.
2. Isaiah 40:8.
3. Daniel 6; Esther 3–8; 1 Samuel 17.
4. Numbers 11:23; Isaiah 59:1.

Chapter 12: Praying for Healing from Eating Disorders and Negative Body Image

1. See Vicki Courtney, *Your Girl: Raising a Godly Daughter in an Ungodly World* (Nashville: Broadman & Holman, 2004), 72.
2. For more information on eating disorders, as well as ways to help your teen, visit www.eatingdisorderhope.com.
3. Ephesians 2:10 NLT.
4. Debra's prayers were rooted in 2 Corinthians 10:4; Romans 12:1–2; and Isaiah 51:16.
5. Psalm 139:13–14; 2 Corinthians 3:18 NLT; Psalm 45:11.
6. Colossians 2:6–8.

Chapter 13: Praying against Self-Harm and Suicide

1. Dennis Thompson, "More American Young People Are Dying by Suicide and Homicide, CDC Reports," CBS News, October 17, 2019, www.cbsnews.com/new /suicide-rate-homicides-rise-american-teens-youth-cdc-reports.
2. Ephesians 4:15.
3. Philippians 1:6.
4. Romans 8:28 NLT.

Chapter 14: Praying through Anxiety and Depression

1. Jonah 4:3 NLT.
2. My paraphrases: Psalm 31:9–12; Ruth 1:20; 1 Kings 19:3–5.
3. Psalm 90:15–16 NLT.
4. Psalm 31:19, 24.

Chapter 15: Praying for Your Teen Rebel

1. Isaiah 53:6.
2. John 10:10 NLT.
3. Psalm 18:16.
4. John 10:10.
5. 1 Corinthians 13:4–7.

6. 2 Corinthians 5:20 NLT.

7. 1 Thessalonians 5:17.

Chapter 16: Praying about Technology and Social Media

1. Mayo Clinic Staff, "Teens and Social Media Use: What's the Impact?" Mayo Clinic, December 21, 2019, www.mayoclinic .org/healthy-lifestyle/tween-and-teen-health/in-depth /teens-and-social-media-use/art-20474437.

2. Andy Crouch, *The Tech-Wise Family: Everyday Steps for Putting Technology in Its Proper Place* (Grand Rapids: Baker, 2017), 26–27.

3. Crouch, *Tech-Wise Family*, 26.

4. For more on this, see Kelly Burch, "How Social Media Affects the Mental Health of Teenagers," *Insider*, March 16, 2020, www.insider.com/how-does-social-media-affect-teenagers.

5. For statistics, as well as resources to help families use the internet safely, visit www.enough.org.

6. Crouch, *Tech-Wise Family*, 171.

7. Crouch, *Tech-Wise Family*, 204.

8. You can read this story in Nehemiah 4.

9. See Crouch, *Tech-Wise Family*, 41–42.

10. Ephesians 6:17.

11. R. A. Torrey, *How to Pray* (Chicago: Moody, 1900), 33.

12. Nehemiah 4:14.

Chapter 17: Praying for Protection from Drinking

1. Marla's prayers came from Ezekiel 36:26; Jeremiah 24:7; and Romans 13:12.

2. 1 Kings 18:21.

3. Luke 15:11–32.

4. John 15:11.

Notes

Chapter 18: Praying for Sexual Purity

1. Pure Excitement rallies were high-energy, one-night events designed to show teens God's plan for sexual purity.
2. 1 Thessalonians 4:4; 1 Corinthians 6:19–20.
3. Song of Songs 2:7.
4. Genesis 2:25.
5. John 16:7–11.
6. Galatians 6:1 NLT.
7. Acts 26:18.
8. Romans 8:38–39.
9. John 8:1–11.

Chapter 19: Praying for Protection from Drugs

1. "Drug Use Among Youth: Facts and Statistics," National Center for Drug Abuse Statistics, https://drugabusestatistics .org/teen-drug-use.
2. John 12:42–43.
3. Colossians 2:13–14 NLT
4. The idea of "standing in the gap" for someone comes from Ezekiel 22.
5. 2 Corinthians 1:8–11 MSG.
6. *The Book of Common Prayer* (New York: Seabury, 1977), 831.
7. Romans 8:1, 39.

Chapter 21: Praying about Choice of Music

1. See Stacey Anderson, "How Music Actually Affects Your Brain," *Teen Vogue*, May 17, 2017, www.teenvogue.com/story /how-music-actually-affects-your-brain.
2. Colossians 4:3.
3. Revelation 3:20.
4. Proverbs 4:23.
5. Galatians 5:17 NLT.
6. Psalm 116:2 NLT.

7. Psalm 40:2–3.

Chapter 22: Praying about Your Teen's Attire

1. Isaiah 3:18–23.
2. Isaiah 3:16–17.
3. Romans 13:14.
4. Romans 12:2 NLT.
5. 1 Timothy 2:9–10.
6. Philippians 2:3–4.
7. Romans 14:13–15.
8. Romans 12:2.

Chapter 23: Praying for Your Teen Athlete

1. Daniel 3.
2. Daniel 3:17–18.

Chapter 24: Praying for Your Teen's Future

1. Jack Hayford, *Prayer Is Invading the Impossible* (South Plainfield, NJ: Logos, 1977), 92.
2. Mark 12:30.
3. Exodus 20:12.
4. 1 Samuel 1; Genesis 49.
5. Stephen and Alex Kendrick, *The Love Dare for Parents* (Nashville: B&H, 2013), 161.
6. Proverbs 18:21 MSG.
7. Numbers 6:24–26.

Acknowledgments

1. Malachi 3:10.
2. Psalm 90:17 NLT.

Connect with

Jodie

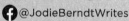

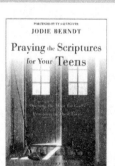

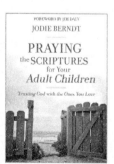

My First 30 Quiet Times

Ty Saltzgiver

Looking for a teen-friendly Bible study?

My First 30 Quiet Times is a powerful
resource for new believers, small group
leaders, and anyone who wants to deepen
their understanding of the Christian faith.
Designed especially for teens, the book features thirty different
topics—knowing God's will, finding freedom from shame, what to do
when suffering comes, dealing with doubt, and more—and has sold
more than 650,000 copies worldwide.

Author Ty Saltzgiver spent more than forty years connecting with
teens through his work with Young Life. A beloved speaker and writer,
Ty makes his home in Colorado Springs, Colorado. He and his wife,
Ann, have three adult sons.